Praise for *The Unofficial Disney Parks Drink Recipe Book*

"If your mind was boggled and your taste buds blown by the sheer creativity, gorgeous photos, and just plain entertaining history and food facts of *The Unofficial Disney Parks Cookbook*, then you will be no less blown away by Ashley Craft's follow-up, *The Unofficial Disney Parks Drink Recipe Book*. From refreshing (Strawberry Acqua Fresca) to unusual (Blurrgfire) to comforting (Black Spire Hot Chocolate) to decadent (Brooklyn Blackout), these drinks evoke the magic and fun of the Disney Parks for young and old and everyone in between. Excuse me while I go into my kitchen to whip up some Frozen Sunshine."
—Dinah Bucholz, author of the *New York Times* bestseller *The Unofficial Harry Potter Cookbook*

Praise for *The Unofficial Disney Parks Cookbook*

"The perfect gift to give your Disney-loving foodie friends for the holidays."
—*Elite Daily*

"The perfect gift this holiday season."
—*Romper*

"Brings the magic of Disney Parks right to your home...
Disney magic and a full belly, does it get better than that?"
—*Laughing Place*

"Just as good as being there."
—*Today.com*

"Sure to satisfy anyone's Disney park cravings....
Will make your family and friends' dreams come true."
—*Reader's Digest*

"Obsessed!"
—*US Weekly*

"Amazing!!"
—*Disabled Disney*

"Like taking a trip without leaving the house."
—*Men's Journal*

"Fantastic!"
—*1StopMom*

"Helps keep the magic alive."
—*Better*

"Better than a FastPass."
—*BuzzFeed*

Adams Media
An Imprint of Simon & Schuster, Inc.
100 Technology Center Drive
Stoughton, Massachusetts 02072

First Adams Media hardcover edition October 2021

ADAMS MEDIA and colophon are trademarks of Simon & Schuster.

For information about special discounts for bulk purchases, please contact Simon & Schuster Special Sales at 1-866-506-1949 or business@simonandschuster.com.

The Simon & Schuster Speakers Bureau can bring authors to your live event. For more information or to book an event contact the Simon & Schuster Speakers Bureau at 1-866-248-3049 or visit our website at www.simonspeakers.com.

Interior design by Sylvia McArdle
Interior photographs by Harper Point Photography
Interior illustrations and maps by Alaya Howard
Interior images © 123RF

Manufactured in the United States of America

1 0 9 8 7 6 5 4 3 2 1

Library of Congress Cataloging-in-Publication Data
Names: Craft, Ashley, author.
Title: The unofficial Disney parks drink recipe book / Ashley Craft.
Description: Stoughton, Massachusetts: Adams Media, 2021. | Series: Unofficial cookbook | Includes index.
Identifiers: LCCN 2021013718 | ISBN 9781507215951 (hc) | ISBN 9781507215968 (ebook)
Subjects: LCSH: Disney, Walt, 1901–1966. | Cooking--California--Disneyland. | Disneyland (Calif.) | LCGFT: Cookbooks.
Classification: LCC TX715.2.C34 C74 2021 | DDC 641.209794/96--dc23
LC record available at https://lccn.loc.gov/2021013718

ISBN 978-1-5072-1595-1
ISBN 978-1-5072-1596-8 (ebook)

The
Unofficial
DISNEY PARKS
DRINK RECIPE
Book

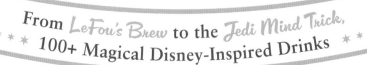

From LeFou's Brew to the Jedi Mind Trick,
100+ Magical Disney-Inspired Drinks

ASHLEY CRAFT

Author of the *USA TODAY* Bestselling *The Unofficial Disney Parks Cookbook*

Adams Media
New York • London • Toronto • Sydney • New Delhi

Dedication

For my kids:
Elliot, Hazel, and Clifford—for going through
the pain and agony of drinking
milkshakes and slushies day after day.
Your sacrifice will bring joy to all
who make these recipes.

Acknowledgments

Thank you to Danny for always treating me like a queen and giving me the confidence to continue writing books.

Thanks to my kids, Elliot, Hazel, and Clifford, for your patience with me as I write and cook. Elliot for "babysitting" the others for me, Hazel for helping me in the kitchen, and Clifford for being by my side all day every day.

I was lucky enough to have Tricia Craft and Emily Goodsell help me edit this book as well as the last one. They both have an amazing eye for good (and bad) writing, and I'm so grateful that they are willing to read my manuscripts over and over and over.

Thank you to my parents, Karen and Jeff Peterson, for rallying around me and the release of *The Unofficial Disney Parks Cookbook*. Your support means everything to me.

Special thank-you to my big sister, Jamie Giles, for taking time away from her family to visit Walt Disney World with me to research this book. And for our poor, unfortunate guts on drinking dozens of specialty drinks....

If you need a literary agent, you'd be blessed to have Joe Perry. His hard work and friendship have meant the world to me this past year.

Contents

Coffee, Tea, Hot Chocolate, & Cider 93

Preface

Nothing quite compares to the feeling of picking up a fun, playful beverage and taking that first sip. The delicious rush of liquid immediately evokes warm memories of great times. A taste of hot apple cider can bring you back to December on a cold day. A gulp of lemonade seems to put the sun into the sky, and you can almost hear the splashes of a summertime pool. But what I love best is the *magic* that comes from partaking of a Disney drink.

Just this year, I visited Walt Disney World Resort in Florida and tasted so many wonderful drinks. I bought the Space Ranger Slushy from Auntie Gravity's in Tomorrowland and sat at a small table watching people dart from Space Mountain to Buzz Lightyear's Space Ranger Spin to the Tomorrowland Speedway. My sister and I sampled many drinks from AbracadaBar at Disney's BoardWalk, and the Hoodunit's Punch blew us away! The enticing blend of fruity flavors was delicious, and I loved the energy in that bar. Memorabilia of magicians lined the walls while bartenders served up drinks that changed color right before our eyes.

A few months later, I made the Hoodunit's Punch for some friends and got to regale them with stories about my trip to Walt Disney World. The combination of sipping and storytelling was such fun. I can't wait to serve up one of these Disney drinks every time I host!

So welcome to my take on the Disney Parks drinks you know and love. Each recipe was lovingly created by me (with the exception of the cocktails, which were concocted by the talented Thea Engst), so you can have a taste of Disney magic right at home.

Introduction

Sparberry Soda, LeFou's Brew, Black Cherry Milkshakes... Disney certainly knows how to make drinks truly special, with over-the-top garnishes and out-of-this-world colors and flavors. Of course, for many, visiting a Disney park to enjoy these treats is an experience that only comes once a year, decade, or even lifetime. Luckily, you can bring the magic of the Disneyland Resort, EPCOT, Disney's Hollywood Studios, Magic Kingdom, Disney's Animal Kingdom, *and* Disney California Adventure right to your kitchen!

The Unofficial Disney Parks Drink Recipe Book includes over one hundred recipes for Disney's most delicious, easy-to-make beverages. Whether you've visited Disney countless times and want to re-create your favorite drinks, or you're looking for something new and Disney-inspired to bring the vacation to you, you're sure to find something that satisfies your taste buds. The recipes are also organized by type of drink, so you can easily flip to whatever fits your mood or occasion. You'll find:

- Fresh lemonades and fruity drinks, like Disney's Hollywood Studios' Moof Juice from a galaxy far, far away and Mystic Portal Punch from Woody's Lunch Box
- Frozen refreshments to beat the heat, including a pink Frozen Flamingo from Harambe Market in Disney's Animal Kingdom and the popular Goofy's Glacier from Goofy's Candy Company in Disney Springs

- Invigorating coffees, teas, ciders, and hot chocolates, like the fan favorite Bubble Milk Tea in EPCOT's China pavilion and the Hot Spiced Apple Cider that can only be found in the lobby of Disney's Grand Californian Hotel & Spa
- Swinging beverages fit for the whole family, including New Orleans Mint Julep mocktails from Disneyland's own New Orleans Square and Zingiber Fizzies from the Nomad Lounge in Disney's Animal Kingdom
- Adult libations like you've never tasted at home before, from a massive Uh Oa! à la Trader Sam's Enchanted Tiki Bar at Disneyland Hotel, to the luxuriant Ice Cream Martini in EPCOT's France pavilion
- And true indulgences, like the Strawberry Shortcake CrazyShake from Black Tap Craft Burgers & Shakes in Downtown Disney and the Minnie Witch Shake from Disney California Adventure's Schmoozies! bar (both decked out with insane toppings!)

These recipes can be the headliner of a spectacular event, a sweet treat for someone special, or the drink you have every morning to start the day—mouse ears optional. Before diving in, just be sure to check out the background information about these drinks in Part 1: Disney Parks Drinks 101, and the details about what tools to have on hand, so you can make the most of each recipe.

Are you ready to bring Disney to your home? As Lumiere would say, "Come on and lift your glass; you've won your own free pass" to stir up some scrumptious liquid magic in the kitchen!

Disney Parks Drinks 101

Whether you always splurge for fancy drinks at Disney, or you bought this book to try these beverages for the first time, welcome to *The Unofficial Disney Parks Drink Recipe Book*!

In this part, you'll explore the drinks of Disney's US parks and resorts, from classics that have been around since the early days of The Walt Disney World Resort, to new favorites and seasonal treasures. Chapter 1 sets the stage for the recipes included in Part 2, giving you some background information about the luscious drinks you'll find in each chapter. Then, before plugging in that blender, you'll want to check out Chapter 2, which details the kitchen tools and syrups necessary to get started. Let's get mixing!

Drinking Around Disney

The Disneyland Resort and Walt Disney World Resort have so much going on, it's hard to get it all done in a single trip. But one thing that should not be missed is the array of varied and wonderful drinks scattered everywhere throughout the parks. Old favorites like the New Orleans Mint Julep and the Dole Whip Float are obviously amazing, but new drinks should also be explored, like the Cliff Dweller from Oga's Cantina (complete with a porg souvenir glass) and the Night Blossom from Pandora—The World of Avatar.

This chapter serves to enhance your enjoyment of Disney, both while at the parks and when mixing up some magic in your own home. Here you'll explore the history of drink offerings at Disney locations, as well as more information on the types of drinks found at each main park. Let's dive in!

The History of Disney Drinks

The Disney experience is not just of the highest quality but is also fully immersive. Guests come not only to enjoy the rides, but to watch shows, appreciate landscaping and design, meet characters, experience amazing smells, listen to music, eat fabulous food, and drink absolutely innovative and invigorating drinks.

Walt Disney originally created Disneyland as an escape that families could take together to enjoy worlds of adventure, fantasy, and the American frontier and the South, along with the promise of tomorrow. Food establishments were sponsored by large corporations, like Hills Bros. Coffee, Welch's, Fritos, Swift & Company, Coca-Cola, Sunkist, and Carnation. These companies worked to peddle their own products and mostly provided provisions made by their own brands. This meant that at the "Casa de Fritos," for example, your only drink options were milk, coffee, or "cold drinks." Any special drinks came from the drink companies themselves. Guests could grab a chilled or frosty grape juice on tap from Welch's Grape Juice Bar, a refreshing glass bottle of Coca-Cola from the Coca-Cola Refreshment Corner, or some fresh-squeezed orange juice from the Sunkist Citrus House. Other than that, specialty drinks weren't really a thing at Disneyland in the 1950s, 1960s, and even 1970s.

Things really started to evolve in the 1980s, when the Dole Company brought the now uber-popular Dole Whip to Disneyland in 1986. Dole Whips were offered in soft serve or float form, so guests could enjoy a deliciously smooth beverage while watching the Tiki Room birds croon. The opening of more table service restaurants like the 50's Prime Time Café in Disney's Hollywood Studios in 1989 brought additional specialty drinks such as Peanut Butter and Jelly Milkshakes and Mickey's Bee Bop Drink.

ALCOHOL IN DISNEY PARKS

In keeping with his vision of family fun, Walt Disney had declared that alcohol would not be sold at Disneyland. He said: "No liquor, no beer, nothing. Because that brings in a rowdy element. That brings people that we don't want, and I feel they don't need it." His wish was kept at Disneyland for sixty-four years.

Walt passed away before Walt Disney World even opened its gates, but his brother Roy honored his legacy and did not permit alcohol to be sold at Magic Kingdom when it was opened. However, when EPCOT Center opened in 1982, the board of executives at Disney decided that in order to fully immerse guests in the countries of the World Showcase, alcohol would have to be served. So alcohol finally came to Disney and continued to be present on opening day for the subsequent three parks (Disney's Hollywood Studios, Disney's Animal Kingdom, and Disney California Adventure). Despite this, it remained banned from Disneyland and Magic Kingdom.

Then, in 2019, Star Wars: Galaxy's Edge opened at Disneyland Park, and with it, Oga's Cantina. This bustling bar pays homage to the Mos Eisley cantina, as seen in *Star Wars: A New Hope*, where Luke Skywalker and Obi-Wan Kenobi meet Han Solo for the first time. Imagineers presumed strong drinks would have been served at the cantina and wanted to bring that spirit to Oga's. So alcohol was introduced to Disneyland. When Bob Iger, president and CEO of the Walt Disney Company at the time, was asked how he so flippantly threw Walt's no-alcohol wishes out the window, he replied: "I think Walt had a nip or two in his [Disneyland] apartment at night."

Today, guests can enjoy family-friendly concoctions like the Hyperdrive (Punch It!) as well as more potent libations like the Jedi Mind Trick. For the first time in Disney Parks history, whole families can sit at a bar together.

The Advent of Events

Over the course of their decades-long history, the Disney Parks have mastered the art of an incredible year-round experience for guests, including seasonal and special offerings. This further entices vacationers to the parks and provides an endless stream of new activities. One such offering is dessert parties. Guests pay a premium price to have a once-in-a-lifetime view of a nighttime show and partake in all-you-care-to-eat desserts and drinks. Usually, the desserts and drinks offered are exclusive to the dessert party, making it all the more desirable.

Another ticketed experience is that of seasonal parties. Each Halloween and Christmas bring parties to the Disneyland Resort and the Walt Disney World Resort, such as the Oogie Boogie Bash, Mickey's Not-So-Scary Halloween Party, and Mickey's Very Merry Christmas Party. These parties really give a lot of bang for the buck with exclusive offerings, including delicious, limited-release drinks. Magical mixes like My Bugs! My Bugs!, Minnie Witch Shake, and Elf Nog can be found at these parties.

Taking the party idea to the next level, EPCOT began holding several festivals every year for the general theme-park public—no extra ticket required. In 1995 the first EPCOT Flower and Garden Festival was held to celebrate springtime and the associated colors and flavors of the season. Also in 1995 was the first EPCOT International Food and Wine Festival. Celebrity chefs and representatives from major food companies come to present stunning dishes to hungry guests. The EPCOT International Festival of the Arts began in 2017 to add performing, visual, and culinary artistry to the festival line-up. Festivals such as these are held each year and cover a lot of the calendar at EPCOT. Booths are scattered throughout the main walkway of the World Showcase, serving up small bites in addition to tantalizing sips. Drinks like Violet Lemonade and Blood Orange Mimosas are just a couple of festival favorites. Those little booths also serve as tiny testing sites for recipes. Many crowd-favorite drink—as well as food—recipes from festivals go on to become permanent menu items at full-time eateries around the Disney Parks. What you sample at a festival may become the next Dole Whip Float!

Events continue to wow park-goers and provide stability year-round for Disney Parks. Ever notice how many festivals and events are at odd times of the year? Like the Walt Disney World Marathon taking place on a random weekend in January? This ensures surges of crowds, even in the "off season." It is a win-win for everyone involved!

The Challenges of Creating a Guest Favorite

While whipping up eye-catching concoctions for Disney Parks may sound like a dream job, Disney chefs take a lot into consideration when creating the latest drink offerings. One of the unexpected considerations is crowd flow. Just as grocers place milk and eggs at the back of the store in order to draw customers through the aisles to get to these essentials, Disney Parks place great care in where the "next big thing" will drop. If they are going to serve a new specialty drink they know will cause a line, they will sell it at a location that can accommodate those crowds.

Another consideration is the latest trends. What flavors are people loving right now? What color palettes are in? How can they make a drink look incredible enough that people will organically post about it on social media? It is not a coincidence that the newest drinks are usually the wildest—like the Poor Unfortunate Souls Float or the insane CrazyShakes of Black Tap. They are made like this to promote free advertisement through photo and video sharing.

And this factor may seem funny but certainly must be addressed: Once people have had plenty to drink at Disney, where can they use the restroom? Disney Parks are well known for their intricate theming and attention to detail. This devotion extends even to the parts of the parks that usually aren't photographed: the bathrooms. Almost every restroom at the Disney Parks has a theme or design unique to itself. Discerning park aficionados have even been known to have favorite bathrooms in each park:

- Disneyland: Star Wars: Galaxy's Edge bathroom for the communal sink trough and Oga's Cantina music.
- Magic Kingdom: Rapunzel bathrooms next to "it's a small world" in homage to all things *Tangled*, including special touches like Maximus's hoof prints.
- EPCOT: Norway bathrooms with the look and feel of Scandinavia, including clean lines and rich colors.

- Disney's Hollywood Studios: The extremely fancy Hollywood Brown Derby restaurant bathrooms right inside the entrance, which allow access to any park-goers.
- Disney's Animal Kingdom: Pandora—The World of Avatar restrooms with beautiful mosaics along the walls.
- Disney California Adventure: The family-friendly Cars Land bathrooms, in case you need to help multiple children at once.

Also, custodians are cleaning these restrooms throughout the day so that a quick time-out to go potty doesn't take away from your magical day.

The last consideration is made by assessing which park is the best "fit" for each treat. For example, in 2021, the movie *Raya and the Last Dragon* premiered. Disney Parks wanted to serve a delicious snack that would get guests excited about the new movie, so they created a dessert called "Baby Tuk Tuk Mousse" that looks like Raya's buddy, Tuk Tuk, transformed into chocolate! Since no parks had any Raya decorations, rides, or theming at the time, Disney executives had to decide where to serve the treat. They landed on Disney's Animal Kingdom, since the film's connection to nature and the "land" of Asia within the park made the most sense. A similar process is made for each new snack, treat, and drink.

Creating Your Own Disney Drinks

Whether you visit Disney Parks frequently, have only been once or twice, or haven't visited yet, this book will help you transform your own kitchen into a magical drink-mixing establishment worthy of a certain mouse. You will soon be whipping up wonderful libations for yourself, friends, and family. But first, be sure to check out the following chapter about essential equipment, syrups, and more before getting started. The delicious world of Disney awaits!

CHAPTER 2

The Disney Mixologist's Essentials

Perhaps you've been whipping up milkshakes and mocktails all your life, or maybe this is your first foray into fine drinks; either way, you'll want to make sure you're prepared with the right equipment and special ingredients for mixing magical recipes. Ice cream makers, blenders, syrups, and more can make the experience as smooth and easy as possible, so you're sipping on a park favorite in no time.

In this chapter, we'll explore everything you need to serve the delicious Disney drinks in Part 2. The tools and ingredient recipes are listed in alphabetical order, so you can easily flip back to a certain section at any time. Once you've taken this closer look, you'll be ready to bust out the blender and start slaying in the kitchen!

Essential Equipment and Pantry Staples

The following are the tools you'll want to have in your kitchen in order to create the recipes in Part 2. Check out your local store or try online retailers. Most (if not all) of this equipment is easy to acquire and doesn't require particular skill to use.

BAKING DISH

For the Frozen Apple Pie recipe you'll need an 8" × 8" baking dish. This can be glass or metal; just be sure it is oven-safe and is greased properly to prevent sticking.

BAKING SHEETS

Baking sheets come in many shapes and sizes, and for the drinks you will be making, it doesn't really matter what kind you use. This book only has three recipes that require baking sheets: Kakamora Floats, Blue Bantha, and Orgeat. For these recipes, cover the baking sheets in parchment paper to prevent sticking.

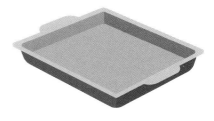

BLENDER

This is the most important tool in this book: Many of the recipes use a blender! You don't need an expensive or fancy blender to make amazing slushes and milkshakes, but the shape does matter. A blender with a funnel-shaped pitcher and a tamper tool (to push ingredients down toward the blade) tends to make the best product, as you don't need to add extra liquids just to blend the drink. Other blenders will work fine, but be sure to stop the blender and stir the ingredients once or twice when blending so as not to burn out the motor. Adding a bit of extra liquid will help if your blender is having trouble making the mixture smooth.

CAKE PANS

The only recipes in this book that need a cake pan are the Kakamora Floats to make cake pops and the Bam Bam Shake to make Fruity Pebbles Bars. Use a 9" × 13" glass or metal pan lined with parchment paper.

CAKE POP STICKS

For the Kakamora Cake Pops, use 6" lollipop sticks. They are typically found in the candy-making section of a grocery or hobby store. If you don't have these on hand, you can use wooden Popsicle sticks.

CHOCOLATE MOLDS

For the Minnie Witch Shake, Mickey Confetti Milkshake, Peter Pan Floats, and Poor Unfortunate Souls Float, chocolate molds are used. You can find these bow- and Mickey-shaped molds through online retailers or at a local hobby store. These creations are just as delicious without the chocolates, so feel free to omit if you desire.

COCKTAIL SHAKER

Many of the recipes call for the use of a cocktail shaker. This makes mixing easy for single-serve mixed drinks, especially if a thicker syrup is used. You can also quickly chill a drink during mixing by adding ice to the shaker. If you don't have a cocktail shaker, just whisk the mixture well in a large glass or small bowl and strain through a sieve.

COFFEE SUBSTITUTE

Some people are not partial to coffee or might want to enjoy a coffee-style beverage later in the day without the surge of caffeine. Many coffee-substitute products are available in stores and provide a natural caffeine- and coffee-free experience. Most are made out of malted barley, chicory, and rye. Pero or Caf-Lib are great choices, as they don't require a coffee machine to brew. Simply follow the instructions on the packaging, then add to the recipe in place of the coffee.

COOKIE SCOOP

The only recipe in this book that uses a cookie scoop is the Kakamora Floats to make cake pops. You should use the smallest cookie scoop you have for this recipe, around 1 tablespoon (the recipe calls for a 1.2-tablespoon size). If you don't have a cookie scoop, a regular spoon is fine, just measure out each spoonful of mixture to about 1 tablespoon.

FOOD COLORING

Many of the recipes use food coloring to pull off the original Disney look. Gel-based colors are always preferred, as they have a brighter pop of color than liquid food coloring, and the tighter consistency won't change the texture of the drink. If your gel colors come in pots and cannot "drop," dip a wooden toothpick into the gel and swipe it through the food or drink you want to color. Repeat with each drop as needed using a fresh toothpick.

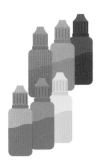

HAWTHORNE STRAINER

This is a type of strainer that you can place on a cocktail shaker or a glass to filter out solids and ice. It is a disc with a handle and stabilizer prongs. If you don't have this particular strainer, you can use a standard sieve.

ICE CREAM MACHINE

Using an ice cream machine for certain slushes is beneficial, since it cuts down on the amount of ice used, which can water down taste. The easiest ice cream machines to use are the ones with freezable bowls. The bowl is removed from the freezer moments before use, and ice cream or drink mix is poured directly into the frozen bowl. The bowl then spins on a base, and a paddle mixes and scrapes the inside. Other options are available if you are unable to use this type of ice cream machine. For example, you can use a bucket-type ice cream machine that requires ice cubes and rock salt. Just pour the mixture from the recipe into the inner metal container and fill the outer bucket with ice and rock salt. Run the machine until the consistency matches the recipe description. If you don't have an ice cream machine, place the liquid mixture in the freezer and stir every 30 minutes until it reaches the desired consistency.

PIPING BAGS

Many recipes in this book call for piping bags, but you don't have to own a fancy set. A heavy-duty plastic sandwich or gallon bag will do nicely. Simply load the whipped cream or other mixture into the bag, then snip a small edge off one of the bottom corners. Start your hole out small and make it bigger as needed.

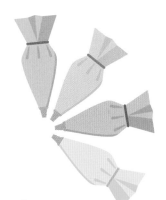

PIPING BAG TIPS

Some recipes call for special piping bag tips, such as a large star tip for certain whipped creams. While you don't need to use a special tip for any recipe, it can make for an eye-catching design.

POTS AND PANS

Heavy-bottomed pots and pans are preferred. The thick metal bottoms regulate the temperature better and prevent burning. If you don't have heavy-bottomed pots and pans, any appropriately sized pot or pan will do; just keep an extra-close eye on foods cooking on the stove. Stir more frequently to prevent burning. Most syrup recipes can be made in a small saucepan.

ROLLING PIN

Rolling pins come in many shapes and sizes, including those that have handles on the sides, French styles, and straight cylindrical styles. Any variety is fine for use in this book. The only recipe requiring a rolling pin is the Bantha Cookies in the Blue Bantha recipe.

SIEVE

The sieve described in the recipes in this book refers to a stainless steel, mesh, half-dome version. It is used to strain out solids and ice. Get one with a fine mesh.

STAND MIXER

This machine makes mixing and whipping easy and uniform. If you don't have a stand mixer, the second-best option is a hand mixer. These often also have changeable attachments for mixing or whipping. Of course, if you have neither, you can simply mix or whip by hand—it will just take a bit more strength and stamina.

Syrups

Syrups are a key part of making many mixed drinks. Disney typically uses the brand Monin for their drinks instead of housemade syrups. This provides consistency and high quality across resorts and is especially useful when drinks change locations—which they often do. Because of this, many of the recipes in this book include ready-made syrups that are relatively easy to obtain in local grocery stores or online. If you can't find a Monin brand, other brands work just as well. Some syrups, however, are harder to find or are particularly easy to make at home. The following recipes are for these kinds of syrups. Any of the recipes in this book can be made using homemade or store-bought syrups—whichever is the best fit for you!

Agave Syrup

YIELDS 2 CUPS

1 cup agave nectar
1 cup water

Combine ingredients in a medium bowl. Store in a medium sealable container in refrigerator up to 1 week.

Black Raspberry Syrup

YIELDS 2 CUPS

1 cup granulated sugar
½ cup fresh or frozen blackberries
½ cup fresh or frozen raspberries
1 tablespoon lemon juice

1. Add ingredients to a small saucepan and mash with a potato masher or wire whisk. Bring to a boil over medium-high heat.

2. Once boiling, remove from heat and allow to cool to room temperature, about 1 hour. Strain into a medium sealable container, discarding solids, and refrigerate at least 1 hour, up to 2 weeks.

Falernum

YIELDS 2 CUPS

1 cinnamon stick
2 tablespoons whole cloves
2 tablespoons ground allspice
1 teaspoon ground nutmeg
4 tablespoons lime juice
2 tablespoons minced ginger
2 cups granulated sugar
1 cup water
½ teaspoon almond extract

1. In a small saucepan over medium heat, toast cinnamon stick, cloves, and allspice until aromatic, about 5 minutes. Place in a blender and blend until ground.

2. In same saucepan over medium-high heat, combine blended spices, nutmeg, lime juice, ginger, sugar, and water. Bring to a boil, then reduce heat to low and simmer 1 minute.

3. Remove from heat, strain into a small sealable container, discarding solids, and allow to cool about 1 hour. Once cooled, squeeze through a cheesecloth into a separate medium sealable container.

4. Add almond extract to mixture. Store in refrigerator up to 2 weeks.

Ginger Syrup

YIELDS 1 CUP

½ cup agave nectar
½ cup water
2 inches gingerroot, peeled and chopped

1. Add all ingredients to a small saucepan. Stir over medium heat until mixture boils.

2. Once boiling, remove from heat and allow to cool about 2 hours. Strain into a small sealable container, discarding solids, and store in refrigerator up to 1 week.

Hibiscus Grenadine

2 cups pomegranate
juice
2 cups granulated sugar
1 cup dried hibiscus
flowers
1 ounce vodka
1 teaspoon orange
blossom water

1. Heat pomegranate juice in a small saucepan over medium heat. Once warm, about 3 minutes, add sugar and stir until sugar is dissolved.

2. Add remaining ingredients. Stir, then bring to a boil.

3. Once boiling, remove from heat and allow to cool, about 2 hours. Strain into a small sealable container, discarding solids, and store in refrigerator up to 1 week.

Kool-Aid Syrup

YIELDS 2 CUPS

1 (0.16-ounce) packet
Kool-Aid Drink Mix
1 cup granulated sugar
1 cup water

1. Combine ingredients in a small saucepan over medium-high heat, stir, and bring to a boil.

2. Once boiling, remove from heat and allow to cool to room temperature, about 1 hour. Pour into a medium sealable container and chill at least 1 hour, up to 4 weeks.

Mint Syrup

YIELDS 1 CUP

1 cup granulated sugar
1 tablespoon mint
 extract
1 cup water

1. Combine ingredients in a small saucepan over medium-high heat, stir, and bring to a boil.

2. Once boiling, remove from heat and allow to cool to room temperature, about 1 hour. Pour into a medium container and chill at least 1 hour, up to 2 weeks.

Orgeat

YIELDS 1½ CUPS

2 cups whole almonds
2 cups granulated sugar
1 cup water

1. Preheat oven to 400°F. Toast almonds on a parchment paper–lined baking sheet 6 minutes. Pour toasted almonds into a blender and pulse until ground.

2. In a medium saucepan over medium-high heat, combine sugar and water and stir 3 minutes. Add ground almonds and stir 3 minutes more. Turn off burner, cover pan, and let steep 3 hours.

3. Strain into a medium container, discarding solids, and refrigerate up to 2 weeks.

Pomegranate Syrup

½ cup pomegranate juice
½ cup granulated sugar

1. Combine ingredients in a small saucepan over medium-high heat, stir, and bring to a boil.

2. Once boiling, remove from heat and allow to cool to room temperature, about 1 hour. Pour into a medium container and chill at least 1 hour, up to 2 weeks.

Red Delicious Apple Syrup

YIELDS 1½ CUPS

1 cup granulated sugar
1 cup cored, peeled, and diced Red Delicious apples
1 tablespoon lemon juice
2 tablespoons thawed apple juice concentrate
2 drops red gel food coloring

1. Combine sugar, apples, and lemon juice in a small saucepan over medium-high heat and mash with a potato masher or wire whisk. Bring to a boil.

2. Once boiling, remove from heat and allow to cool to room temperature, about 1 hour. Strain into a small container, discarding solids, then add apple juice concentrate and food coloring. Chill at least 1 hour, up to 2 weeks.

Ginger Rosemary Simple Syrup

½ cup agave nectar
½ cup water
4 medium sprigs
  rosemary
2 inches gingerroot,
  peeled and chopped

Add all ingredients to a small saucepan. Stir over medium heat until mixture boils. Once boiling, remove from heat and allow to cool about 2 hours. Strain into a small sealable container, discarding solids, and store in refrigerator up to 1 week.

Simple Syrup

1 cup granulated sugar
1 cup water

1. Combine ingredients in a small saucepan over medium-high heat, stir, and bring to a boil.

2. Once boiling, remove from heat and allow to cool to room temperature, about 1 hour. Pour into a medium container and chill at least 1 hour, up to 4 weeks.

Other Mixer Ingredients

Disney Parks are known for having eye-catching and tongue-teasing drinks, and those are sometimes achieved by having some strange ingredients. The following three recipes are included in that category. They will take your drinks above and beyond!

Buzz Button Tingling Foam

YIELDS 2 CUPS

For Buzz Button Tingling Syrup

20 large Szechuan buttons
1 cup granulated sugar
1 cup water

For Foam

4 ounces heavy whipping cream
2 ounces Buzz Button Tingling Syrup

1. To make Syrup: Muddle Szechuan buttons in a large bowl.

2. Combine sugar and water in a small saucepan over medium heat, and stir until sugar has dissolved.

3. Stir in Szechuan buttons. Bring to a boil over medium heat, then remove from heat. Cover and refrigerate overnight. Strain into a medium sealable container, discarding solids. Store in refrigerator up to 1 week.

4. To make Foam: Remove Hawthorne strainer from a cocktail shaker and add ingredients. Shake until liquid solidifies. Store in a small sealable container in refrigerator up to 3 days.

Hibiscus Salt

YIELDS 2½ TABLESPOONS

1½ tablespoons salt
1 tablespoon dried
  hibiscus flowers

Muddle ingredients together in a small bowl until salt turns purple. Store in a small sealable container at room temperature up to 3 days.

Sam's Gorilla Grog

YIELDS 6½ OUNCES

3 ounces passion-
  orange-guava juice
2 ounces lemon juice
1 ounce pineapple juice
¼ ounce Falernum (see
  recipe in this chapter)
¼ ounce Orgeat (see
  recipe in this chapter)

Shake all ingredients in a sealed cocktail shaker. Strain into a medium sealable container and store in refrigerator up to 2 weeks.

Getting Started

Now that you've explored the main tools, syrups, and other special ingredients you'll want to have on hand, you are ready to get mixing! Remember: Although these recipes are modeled after Disney Park originals, the drinks you create are unique to your tastes. Experiment with your favorite flavors, try different designs where applicable, use the glasses you have on hand, and have fun with it. When in doubt, refer back to the kitchen essentials information in this chapter. It's time to whip up some delicious magic!

PART 2

Delicious Drinks

It's the moment you've been waiting for: the recipes! You've learned all about Disney Parks and their past, present, and in-the-works takes on delicious beverages. You've studied all the equipment you need to master each recipe ahead. You're ready to start mixing!

In the following chapters, you will find over one hundred beautiful, luscious beverages inspired by the classic and modern favorites at Disney's six US parks and their surrounding hotels and attractions. The chapters are organized by type of drink, so you can flip through to whatever fits your mood. From refreshing lemonades and family-friendly mocktails to adult libations and indulgent dessert drinks, there's something for every occasion. You are likely to find drinks you have tasted at the Disney Parks, but you may also discover recipes you've never heard of or seen before. Give these a try! You never know what will become your next go-to. Also, remember that you are the master of your own kitchen: experiment and substitute flavors in and out as your heart desires. Maybe your creation will be the next sensation! Read on and be transported to a whole new world!

CHAPTER 3

Lemonades & Fruity Drinks

Southern California and Central Florida are known for being hot a good portion of the year. In fact, this is one reason why Walt Disney chose to put his parks there—so they could remain open year-round. But because of this, guests are constantly needing to stay hydrated as they walk miles upon miles each day to check out all the parks have to offer. This need has led to the creation of some of the most popular beverages across all Disney Parks.

And now you can skip the lines and quench your thirst without leaving home! This chapter is full of refreshing lemonades and fruity drinks you'll keep flipping back to. Give Mystic Portal Punch from Toy Story Land a try (little green man not included), or perhaps branch out to try more exotic flavors like the Popping Yuzu Lemonade sold at Disney Springs. And why have a plain ol' lemonade when you can have the green Keiki Lemonade from Tambu Lounge at Disney's Polynesian Village Resort?! Magical recipes await.

Bibo

Harambe Market, Disney's Animal Kingdom

· · · ✦ · · ·

Unlike most drinks sold at Disney, this beverage is not a creation of the Walt Disney Company. Bibo is a regional soda made by the Coca-Cola Company that was previously sold in South Africa and Mozambique, as well as a few other countries. The drink came in a variety of flavors with wild names: Candy Pine-Nut, Johnny Orange, Paolo Peach, Taka Strawberry, Jay Apple, and DJ Kiwi Mango. They all sound delicious! This is an approximation of the flavors of the Bibo sold in Harambe Market.

SERVES 1

8 ounces Mountain Berry Blast Powerade
1 ounce rock melon cantaloupe syrup
2 ounces kiwi syrup

Add all ingredients to a cocktail shaker half full of ice, seal, and shake until well mixed. Pour into a 16-ounce plastic cup or glass and fill with ice.

Blood Orange (Virgin) Mimosa

Shimmering Sips, EPCOT

· · · ✦ · · ·

Shimmering Sips is one of the delightful booths available at the EPCOT International Food and Wine Festival. Park-goers can find an assortment of small buildings scattered throughout the World Showcase, featuring either a specific country's cuisine or a specific food or drink item (such as at Shimmering Sips!). Mimosas are typically made with sparking alcoholic wine and are served with breakfast or brunch. This version is alcohol-free so the whole family can enjoy!

SERVES 1

½ cup sparkling white grape juice
½ cup blood orange juice with pulp

Pour grape juice into a champagne glass and top with blood orange juice.

Cotton Candy Lemonade *(pictured)*

AbracadaBar, Disney's BoardWalk

· · · ✳ · · ·

If you don't own cotton candy syrup, try this hack! You can use cotton candy sugar (usually available at grocery stores) to make a simple syrup: Just pour 1 cup cotton candy sugar and 1/2 cup water into a small saucepan and bring to a boil over medium heat. Once boiling, remove from heat, stir well, and keep cooled until ready to use. If you'd like to just buy cotton candy syrup, try online retailers. They typically ship free and quickly!

SERVES 1

8 ounces lemonade
2 ounces cotton candy
  syrup
1 maraschino cherry

Pour lemonade and cotton candy syrup into a cocktail shaker half full of ice, seal, and shake well. Pour into a 16-ounce glass and fill with ice. Garnish with maraschino cherry.

Tropical Breeze Smoothie

Oasis Sweets & Sips, EPCOT

· · · ✳ · · ·

If you're looking for a fruity burst of fresh flavor, look no further. This smoothie is almost entirely sweetened by natural fruits and has no artificial flavors. The combination of bananas, peaches, and mangoes transports the drinker to a tropical place. It would also make a lovely addition to any breakfast!

SERVES 1

1 cup frozen banana slices
1 cup frozen peach slices
1 1/4 cups mango nectar
1 ounce Simple Syrup (see
  recipe in Chapter 2)

Add ingredients to a blender and pulse until well mixed. Pour into a 20-ounce plastic cup or glass and serve immediately.

Blood Orange Acqua Fresca

Via Napoli Ristorante e Pizzeria, EPCOT

· · · ✦ · · ·

Blood oranges are a specific variety of orange usually only available between December and April. If you happen to want a Blood Orange Acqua Fresca sometime between May and November, here's a little hack: Use navel oranges instead of blood oranges and add ½ cup fresh raspberries to the recipe. This will mimic some of the raspberry flavor tones blood oranges naturally carry and give it a deeper color as well!

SERVES 4

2 cups peeled and
segmented blood
oranges
4 cups water, divided
½ cup granulated sugar
4 blood orange wheels

1. Combine blood orange segments, ½ cup water, and sugar in a small bowl and chill in refrigerator 4 hours.

2. Pour chilled mixture into a blender and pulse until well puréed. Strain into a pitcher, discarding solids, and add remaining 3½ cups water. Stir well.

3. Pour into four regular drinking glasses over ice and garnish each with 1 blood orange wheel. Leftovers can be refrigerated up to 5 days.

Frozen Flamingo

Harambe Market, Disney's Animal Kingdom

· · · ✳ · · ·

This beverage used to be offered in an Ocarina Musical Sipper cup, which featured a playable flute on the handle. I'm sure every parent regretted the decision to buy that cup! Whether it is served in a fancy sipper or simple plastic cup, this smoothie-like beverage is sure to cool you down on a hot day.

SERVES 1

1½ cups frozen
strawberries
1 cup passion fruit juice
1 ounce passion fruit
syrup

Add all ingredients to a blender and blend until smooth. Pour into a 16-ounce plastic cup or glass and serve immediately.

Jungle Juice

Boma—Flavors of Africa, Disney's Animal Kingdom Lodge

· · · ✳ · · ·

If the ingredients for Jungle Juice sound familiar, it's because they are the ingredients for the popular Hawaiian beverage known as POG. "POG" stands for passion fruit, orange, and guava. Disney decided to rebrand this common drink and serve it in many restaurants and quick-service locations around the Walt Disney World Resort. It's easy to make using the following recipe, but you can also check the refrigerated section of your grocery store for a prebottled version. Just look for "passion fruit, orange, guava," not Jungle Juice!

SERVES 1

1 cup pulp-free orange
juice
1 cup passion fruit juice
1 cup guava nectar

Pour orange juice, passion fruit juice, and guava nectar into a tall drinking glass. Stir and serve.

Frozen Sunshine *(pictured)*

Beaches & Cream Soda Shop, Disney's Beach Club Resort

· · · ✦ · · ·

If you could trap sunshine and put it in a glass, this would be it. Highlighting the orange flavors of the Sunshine State (Florida!), this drink will have you believing you are sipping a Creamsicle right through a straw! The candy orange slice garnish adds a bit of whimsy to this recipe. Have your sunglasses nearby while you drink this one!

SERVES 2

½ cup orange soda
1 cup orange sherbet
1 cup vanilla ice cream
½ cup whipped cream
4 orange slice candies

1. In a blender, combine orange soda, orange sherbet, and ice cream until well mixed.

2. Pour into two tall drinking glasses and top each with ¼ cup whipped cream. Place 2 orange slice candies gently on top of each scoop of whipped cream. Serve immediately.

Mickey's Bee Bop Drink

50's Prime Time Café, Disney's Hollywood Studios

· · · ✦ · · ·

Although this drink may seem like a simple Shirley Temple, it actually isn't! Shirley Temple drinks are made with grenadine syrup. Most people believe grenadine is cherry flavored, but in fact it is made with pomegranate juice and sugar. So even though Shirley Temples are garnished with cherries, the drink itself is not cherry. This version is served at 50's Prime Time Café in a kid's cup with a Disney glow cube.

SERVES 1

8 ounces lemon-lime soda
1½ ounces cherry syrup
1 maraschino cherry

Pour lemon-lime soda and cherry syrup into a regular drinking glass. Stir, fill with ice, and garnish with maraschino cherry.

Lava Smoothie

Leaping Horse Libations, Disney's BoardWalk Villas

. . . ✦ . . .

The combination of raspberry and pineapple in this smoothie is a delightful surprise. Both are known for their tartness, and blending them together with coconut flavors creates a super-refreshing beverage. Imagine you are sitting next to the incredible Disney's BoardWalk Inn roller coaster water slide while sipping this drink.

SERVES 2

½ cup fresh or frozen raspberries
½ cup granulated sugar
1 tablespoon lemon juice
8 ounces nonalcoholic piña colada mix
2 ounces pineapple juice
3 cups crushed ice
2 pineapple wedges

1. Mash raspberries, sugar, and lemon juice in a small saucepan over medium heat. Once mixture just begins to boil, remove from heat. Strain into a small sealable container, discarding solids, and chill 1 hour.

2. In a blender, combine piña colada mix, pineapple juice, and ice. Blend until slushy. Split between two 16-ounce drinking glasses or plastic cups. Divide raspberry purée evenly between glasses, pouring on top of the piña colada slush. Gently blend with a spoon, while keeping visible swirls, and serve garnished with pineapple wedges.

Keiki Lemonade

Tambu Lounge, Disney's Polynesian Village Resort

· · · ✦ · · ·

Who knew lemonade could be green?! The blend of yellow and orange colors, when mixed with the blue curaçao syrup, turns this drink green! It is ultra-refreshing after a long day at Magic Kingdom, and is just as refreshing after a long hard day at home or work. Just imagine sitting at the bar of Tambu Lounge while you mix this up at your kitchen table.

SERVES 1

6 ounces lemonade
1 ounce pulp-free orange juice
2 ounces pineapple juice
2 ounces passion fruit juice
½ ounce alcohol-free blue curaçao syrup
2 pineapple wedges

Add all ingredients to a cocktail shaker half full of ice, seal, and shake well. Pour into a regular drinking glass or goblet, fill with ice, and garnish with pineapple wedges.

Sparberry Soda

Harambe Market, Disney's Animal Kingdom

· · · ✦ · · ·

This soda is actually a canned or fountain beverage manufactured by the Coca-Cola Company in South Africa. Made by Sparletta, other varieties sold in African countries include Crème Soda, Pine Nut, Iron Brew, and Apple Rush. Luckily for residents of other countries, the flavors of Sparberry Soda are easy to replicate at home with cream soda and some fresh raspberries.

SERVES 1

½ cup fresh raspberries
12 ounces cream soda

In a large glass, muddle raspberries into cream soda. Strain into a 16-ounce plastic cup or glass and discard solids. Fill with ice.

Mixed Berries Delight

Oasis Sweets & Sips, EPCOT

*   *   *   ✦   *   *   *

If you're a berry fan, this drink is for you. A delicious combination of strawberries, raspberries, and blueberries is perfectly blended with apple juice. If you don't have separate bags of the frozen berries available, you can buy a bag of mixed berries and simply add 1 cup of that mix to the blender. Each time you make it, it will have a slightly different composition of berries!

SERVES 1

4 ounces apple juice
½ ounce lime juice
⅓ cup frozen strawberries
⅓ cup frozen raspberries
⅓ cup frozen blueberries
1 ounce Simple Syrup (see recipe in Chapter 2)

Add all ingredients to a blender and blend until smooth. Pour into a 16-ounce plastic cup or glass and serve with a straw.

Mystic Portal Punch

Woody's Lunch Box, Disney's Hollywood Studios

*   *   *   ✦   *   *   *

This drink is typically served in a souvenir cup complete with a three-eyed alien and arcade grabber claw! For a DIY version, simply glue a Toy Story alien action figure to the bottom of a clear tumbler using a food-safe adhesive. It will be covered up by the opaque liquid and discovered by the drinker when they get to the bottom!

SERVES 1

4 ounces pulp-free tangerine juice
6 ounces Mountain Berry Blast Powerade
3 ounces lemon-lime soda

Combine tangerine juice, Powerade, and lemon-lime soda in a clear plastic or glass tumbler. Fill with ice and serve.

Moof Juice

Docking Bay 7 Food and Cargo, Disneyland and Disney's Hollywood Studios

· · · ✦ · · ·

Docking Bay 7 has some of the most delicious quick-service meals in all the Disney Parks. This Moof Juice is no exception. Although subtle, the chipotle-pineapple syrup adds a depth of flavor that truly feels alien—and delicious. The roof of Docking Bay 7 holds a freighter delivering cargo marked with some interesting numbers: 77, 80, 83. These are the years each of the original Star Wars movies were released!

SERVES 1

4 ounces fruit punch
4 ounces pulp-free orange juice
2 ounces pineapple juice
½ ounce chipotle-pineapple syrup

Add all ingredients to a cocktail shaker half full of ice, seal, and shake well. Pour into a 16-ounce plastic cup or glass and fill with ice.

MIX IT UP

If chipotle in a drink doesn't sound like the flavor you're looking for, use plain pineapple syrup instead. If you don't have any on hand, make some by mashing 1 cup pineapple chunks, 1 cup granulated sugar, and 1 tablespoon lemon juice in a small saucepan over medium heat until boiling, then strain into a small container, discarding solids, and let cool completely.

Pandoran Sunrise

Satu'li Canteen, Disney's Animal Kingdom

· · · ✦ · · ·

If you find yourself feeling tired and drained, give yourself a break by whipping up a Pandoran Sunrise. The blend of fruit juices and exotic flavors will have you yelling *"Sivako!"* or "Rise to the challenge!" in Na'vi.

SERVES 1

6 ounces pineapple juice
4 ounces mango juice
1 ounce rock melon cantaloupe syrup
½ ounce lime juice
1 pineapple wedge

Combine pineapple juice, mango juice, cantaloupe syrup, and lime juice in a cocktail shaker half full of ice, seal, and shake well. Pour into a 16-ounce plastic cup or glass, fill with ice, and garnish with pineapple wedge.

Pomegranate Lemonade

Tambu Lounge, Disney's Polynesian Village Resort

· · · ✦ · · ·

In 2020 and 2021, Disney's Polynesian Village Resort underwent an extensive renovation to re-theme some segments to *Moana*. As one of the original 1971 hotels, it has transformed many times over the years, but the beauty and feel that Walt Disney imagined for it has always delivered. If you get the chance to stay at the Polynesian Resort, make a stop at Tambu Lounge. Grab a drink from the bar and settle down in a squashy chair to enjoy it. Or make this drink at home and sit in your own squashy chair!

SERVES 1

6 ounces lemonade
2 ounces pomegranate juice
½ ounce lime juice

Combine all ingredients in a cocktail shaker half full of ice, seal, and shake well. Pour into a regular drinking glass or goblet and fill with ice.

Strawberry Acqua Fresca

Via Napoli Ristorante e Pizzeria, EPCOT

* * * ✦ * * *

Acqua fresca literally translates to "fresh water" in Italian, so don't be surprised that the flavors of this beverage are light and bright. Unlike heavy juices or sodas, Acqua Frescas are mostly composed of fresh fruit and water, with just a bit of sugar to add some sweetness. At Via Napoli, several flavors of Acqua Fresca are on display in gigantic dispensers. It's hard not to try every flavor!

SERVES 4

2 cups hulled and quartered fresh strawberries
4 cups water, divided
½ cup granulated sugar
4 whole fresh strawberries, slit up center

1. Combine quartered strawberries, ½ cup water, and sugar in a large bowl and refrigerate 4 hours.

2. Pour chilled mixture into a blender and pulse until well puréed. Strain into a pitcher, discarding solids, and add remaining 3½ cups water. Stir well.

3. Pour into four regular drinking glasses or goblets and garnish each with a whole strawberry on the rim. Leftovers can be refrigerated up to 5 days.

Popping Yuzu Lemonade

YeSake Kiosk, Disney Springs

· · · ✦ · · ·

Yuzu is an East Asian citrus variety that looks like a wrinkly orange, with juice that tastes like a mix of grapefruit and mandarin orange juice. The sweet-and-sour flavor is similar to that of a lemon but provides a fun change from typical lemonade. Yuzu can be found in some Asian grocery stores or ordered online.

SERVES 4

¾ cup granulated sugar
4 cups water, divided
1 cup yuzu juice
¾ cup lemon juice
1 cup popping pearls
  (mango, strawberry, or
  blueberry), including
  juices, divided
4 lemon wheels

1. In a small saucepan over medium heat, add sugar and ½ cup water. Stir frequently and remove from heat once it just begins to boil. Chill 1 hour.

2. Add remaining 3½ cups water, yuzu juice, and lemon juice to chilled mixture. Divide into four 16-ounce plastic cups or glasses. Top each glass with ice until nearly full and ¼ cup popping pearls, including juices. Add large gauge straws, lemon wheels, and serve.

MIX IT UP

If you can't get ahold of yuzu juice, just replace the 1 cup yuzu juice in this recipe with ½ cup grapefruit juice and ½ cup mandarin orange juice. The combination has a similar flavor profile, and both juices can be found in most grocery stores.

Ramone's "Pear of Dice" Soda *(pictured)*

Cozy Cone Motel, Disney California Adventure

* * * ✦ * * *

If you're looking for a sweet sip, you're in the right place. The desert pear syrup lends an original and unexpected flavor to this popping pink beverage. Inspired by the character Ramone from the Cars movie franchise, it fits right into Cars Land in Disney California Adventure. But did you know that the original storyline of *Cars* was actually meant to be about an electric car with an "ugly duckling" redemption arc? It would make for a very different personality for Lightning McQueen!

SERVES 1

1 ounce nonalcoholic mojito mix
1 ounce desert pear syrup
12 ounces lemon-lime soda

Stir together mojito mix, desert pear syrup, and lemon-lime soda in a 16-ounce plastic cup or glass. Fill with ice.

The Red Maple

Le Cellier Steakhouse, EPCOT

* * * ✦ * * *

If you want to grab this drink the next time you're at Walt Disney World, you'll also need to grab a coveted reservation at one of the resort's most popular restaurants, Le Cellier Steakhouse. Located in the Canada pavilion in EPCOT, Le Cellier treats guests to luscious Canadian dishes like Beef Bourguignon Poutine, Canadian Cheddar Cheese Soup, and Maple Crème Brûlée. This drink has been known to come and go from the Le Cellier menu. Luckily, it's easy to make at home with just two simple ingredients.

SERVES 1

3 cups raspberry sorbet
¾ cup lemon-lime soda

Add ingredients to a blender and pulse until well mixed. Pour into a regular drinking glass or goblet and serve immediately.

Spooky Apple Punch

Flame Tree Barbecue, Disney's Animal Kingdom

· · · · ✦ · · ·

A seasonal offering available at Flame Tree Barbecue in September and October, this drink is very much like a green apple Shirley Temple. The familiar fizzy taste of the lemon-lime soda is beautifully matched to the sour apple syrup. It's a new twist on an old classic. Adding the sugar-lime rim and Candy-Coated Straw really takes this drink to the next level—but you don't have to add them if you don't want to. This drink looks great at a fun Halloween party, or just being glugged on a Tuesday at home! Complete the effect with an official Disney glow cube.

SERVES 1

For Punch
½ small lime
1 teaspoon lime zest
1 tablespoon granulated sugar
1½ ounces Granny Smith apple syrup
8 ounces lemon-lime soda

For Candy-Coated Straw
3 green apple Jolly Rancher candies
3 green apple Life Savers candies, crushed

For Garnish
1 gummy worm

1. To make Punch: Rub rim of a 16-ounce plastic cup or glass with lime. Stir together lime zest and sugar in a shallow dish and dip rim of glass in zest and sugar mix. Twist in sugar to coat rim.

2. Pour apple syrup and lemon-lime soda into the prepared glass.

3. To make Candy-Coated Straw: Microwave Jolly Ranchers on high 1 minute in a small microwave-safe bowl. Pour crushed Life Savers into a shallow dish. Use a butter knife to smooth melted Jolly Ranchers onto the outside of a plastic straw, then quickly roll the straw in Life Savers.

4. To serve: Add ice to Punch to fill glass, then add Candy-Coated Straw and gummy worm. Serve.

CHAPTER 4

Slushes

Disney has perfected the art of slush making. Most of their restaurants and snack stands have big slush mixers that are constantly spinning and keeping drinks perfectly frozen and ready to drink. Most of us don't have equipment like that in our kitchens, but having a perfect slush is not an impossible feat! The recipes in this chapter have been formulated with the home cook in mind, to enable you to make incredible frozen beverages using simple, everyday tools.

Have you heard of the beloved Blue and Green Milks that are served at the Milk Stand in Star Wars: Galaxy's Edge at both Disneyland and Disney's Hollywood Studios? Well, you won't need the Force to make these iconic drinks at home. And you can enjoy seasonal favorites any time of the year, with Halloween treats like My Bugs! My Bugs! and Witch's Frozen Brew, and winter magic like the Sleigh-Ride Slush. In your own home, *you* make the rules!

Blue Milk

. . . ✦ . . .

Few things have divided Disney fans like the debate between the two milks: Blue and Green. Which do you prefer? Some visitors to Star Wars: Galaxy's Edge have thrown the argument out the window by layering the two milks together in one cup! The fruity and floral flavors of both milks blend together perfectly for your taste buds to enjoy. You can find the recipe for Green Milk in this chapter and try this method yourself!

SERVES 2

½ cup rice milk
½ cup unsweetened canned coconut milk
1 cup pineapple juice
½ cup passion fruit juice
1 tablespoon lime juice
1 tablespoon watermelon syrup
2 drops blue gel food coloring

1. In a blender, add all ingredients and blend until smooth.

2. Pour mixture into an ice cream machine. Follow manufacturer's instructions and run about 8 minutes until slushy.

3. Pour into two regular drinking glasses and enjoy immediately.

Wonderland Slushy

Cheshire Café, Magic Kingdom

· · · ✦ · · ·

The Wonderland Slushy is named after the mythical land described in Lewis Carroll's *Alice's Adventures in Wonderland*. Alice falls down a rabbit hole and winds up in a magical place where nothing is as it seems. Grape and raspberry aren't flavors that typically get paired together in this world, but maybe they are commonplace in Wonderland. Just be sure not to get tricked by the Queen of Hearts: She's probably going to try to sneak a sip of this from you!

SERVES 1

For Slushy
4 ounces grape Kool-Aid Syrup (see recipe in Chapter 2)
1 ounce club soda
3 cups crushed ice, divided
3 ounces raspberry lemonade
2 ounces Simple Syrup (see recipe in Chapter 2)

For Candy-Coated Straw
3 cherry Jolly Rancher candies
2 cherry Life Savers candies, crushed
1 grape Life Savers candy, crushed

1. To make Slushy: Add Kool-Aid Syrup, club soda, and 1½ cups ice to a blender and blend until smooth. Pour into a medium bowl and set aside. Rinse out blender.

2. Add raspberry lemonade, Simple Syrup, and remaining 1½ cups ice to blender and blend until smooth. Layer grape and raspberry slushes in a 16-ounce plastic cup or glass.

3. To make Candy-Coated Straw: Microwave Jolly Ranchers on high 1 minute in a small microwave-safe bowl. Pour crushed Life Savers into a shallow dish and toss to mix up colors. Use a butter knife to smooth melted Jolly Ranchers three-quarters of the way up the length of a plastic straw, then quickly roll straw in Life Savers. Add to slush (exposed side down) and serve.

Goofy's Glacier

Goofy's Candy Company, Disney Springs

· · · ✦ · · ·

These sweet slushes can be found at Big Top Treats in Magic Kingdom or at Goofy's Candy Company at Disney Springs. The flavors change frequently, but some guest favorites include Orange You Happy Orange, Pucker Purple, Gawrshly Berry Blue, and Rootin' Tootin' Red. Try mixing several flavors together to create a new combination that you are the first person to try!

SERVES 1

8 ounces any flavor Kool-Aid Syrup (see recipe in Chapter 2)
2 ounces club soda
3 cups crushed ice

Add Kool-Aid Syrup, club soda, and ice to a blender and blend until smooth. Pour into a 20-ounce plastic cup or glass and serve immediately.

MIX IT UP

Using Kool-Aid to make syrups offers a wide range of flavors. Feel free to try any of your favorite flavors when making a Goofy's Glacier!

Green Milk

Milk Stand, Disneyland and Disney's Hollywood Studios

. . . ✦ . . .

Green Milk sold at Disneyland and Disney's Hollywood Studios is a plant-based concoction with a flowery taste. However, the "real" story behind Green Milk is that it is milked from female thala-sirens. These creatures are famously found on Ahch-To (where Luke Skywalker hid himself for years) but also live on Batuu. Bubo Wamba Family Farms procures and bottles the stuff and ships it to the Milk Stand at Black Spire Outpost to sell to thirsty customers. Mmm, refreshing!

SERVES 2

½ cup rice milk
½ cup unsweetened canned coconut milk
1 cup pulp-free orange juice
1 cup passion fruit juice
¼ cup light corn syrup
3 drops lime-green gel food coloring

1. Add all ingredients to a blender and blend until smooth.

2. Pour mixture into an ice cream machine. Follow manufacturer's instructions and run about 5–10 minutes until slushy.

3. Pour into two regular drinking glasses and enjoy immediately.

Habibi Daiquiri

Oasis Sweets & Sips, EPCOT

. . . ✦ . . .

The word *habibi* translates to "my love" or "darling" in Arabic. Whether you're having a romantic stroll around the World Showcase at EPCOT or simply enjoying the company of someone you love at home, why not share a nice Habibi Daiquiri? One of the best views of EPCOT nighttime spectaculars is from the Morocco pavilion. Re-create this at home by playing *Illuminations* on your TV. Habibi Daiquiri + two straws + *Illuminations* = date night covered!

SERVES 1

2 ounces sweet and sour mix
2 ounces white grape juice
2 ounces strawberry syrup
2 cups crushed ice
2 ounces blood orange Italian soda

Add sweet and sour mix, grape juice, strawberry syrup, and ice to a blender. Blend until smooth. Pour into a 16-ounce plastic cup or glass and top with blood orange soda. Stir gently and serve.

MIX IT UP

If you can't get ahold of blood orange Italian soda to make this at home, you can trade it out for any other sparkling beverage. Give lemon-lime soda, flavored sparkling water, or plain club soda a try!

LeFou's Brew

Gaston's Tavern, Magic Kingdom

· · · ✦ · · ·

If you are a California native, the ingredients for this drink might sound familiar to you. The same beverage is sometimes sold at Disney California Adventure under a different name! Pick up Red's Apple Freeze from Cozy Cone Motel in Cars Land for a taste of LeFou's Brew on the opposite coast. Hey, it's a delicious drink: The more places they can sell it, the better! And now this easy-to-make recipe can bring LeFou's Brew to your home, wherever you may be.

SERVES 3

1 cup heavy whipping
  cream
3 tablespoons mango
  juice
3 tablespoons passion
  fruit juice
¼ cup powdered sugar
1 (12-ounce) can frozen
  apple juice concentrate
3 cups cold water
3 tablespoons toasted
  marshmallow syrup

1. In the bowl of a stand mixer, combine cream, mango juice, passion fruit juice, and sugar. Using the whisk attachment, whip until soft peaks form. Cover and refrigerate fruit foam while completing next steps.

2. In a large bowl, mix apple juice concentrate with water. Add toasted marshmallow syrup and mix. Pour apple juice mixture into an ice cream machine. Follow manufacturer's instructions and run 10 minutes.

3. Scoop apple juice mixture into three 16-ounce plastic cups or glasses and top evenly with fruit foam. Discard or save any extra foam. Stir a bit to blend flavors before sipping.

Moroccarita

Oasis Sweets & Sips, EPCOT

· · · ✦ · · ·

If you get the chance to visit the Morocco pavilion at EPCOT, take a few moments to appreciate the beauty of the architecture and art there. Due to Islamic beliefs on the content of art, you'll find no people represented in any of the mosaics throughout the pavilion. The Moroccan government had actually operated the pavilion since its opening in 1984 but gave up control in late 2020.
This drink is a twist on a classic margarita and is made
without alcohol so the whole family can enjoy!

SERVES 1

4 ounces nonalcoholic margarita mix
4 ounces lemon-lime soda
2 ounces pulp-free orange juice
1 ounce Simple Syrup (see recipe in Chapter 2)
½ ounce lime juice
2 cups crushed ice

Add all ingredients to a blender. Blend until smooth. Pour into a 16-ounce plastic cup or glass and serve immediately.

Jungle Julep

Bengal Barbecue, Disneyland

· · · ✦ · · ·

Although this fruity frozen drink goes great with barbecued skewers, it can be enjoyed with any meal. The addition of the pineapple leaf and orange slice garnishes takes it to the next level. Let's brush up on your Jungle Cruise jokes so you can say them at home: "There's my favorite crocodile, Ginger. But watch out.... Ginger snaps!" "This is Schweitzer Falls. Named after the famous explorer Albert Falls." Top your drinks with colorful drink umbrellas and unwind.

SERVES 2

2 cups frozen pineapple chunks
1 cup pulp-free orange juice
1 cup 100% grape juice
¼ cup lemon juice
2 tablespoons granulated sugar
2 pineapple leaves
2 orange slices

Add pineapple chunks, orange juice, grape juice, lemon juice, and sugar to a blender and blend until smooth. Pour into two 16-ounce plastic cups or glasses. Garnish each glass with a pineapple leaf and orange slice. Serve immediately.

Pirate Pear Slushy

Tortuga Tavern, Magic Kingdom

· · · ✦ · · ·

If you've never had desert pear or prickly pear flavor before, you're in for a real treat. It has notes of strawberry and raspberry but is extra-sweet like bubble gum. It really is a unique flavor, and it's worth having the syrup around the house! Tortuga Tavern is only open seasonally at Magic Kingdom, so if you see it open, be sure to complement your Pirate Pear Slushy with a barbecue sandwich!

SERVES 1

4 ounces lemon-lime soda
2 ounces desert pear syrup
2 cups crushed ice

Add all ingredients to a blender and blend until smooth. Pour into a 16-ounce plastic cup or glass and serve immediately.

Pomegranate-Lime Frozen Virgin Mojito

La Cantina de San Angel, EPCOT

· · · ✦ · · ·

Origins of the mojito are traced back to Cuba in the 1600s, when locals would use this rum, lime, and mint beverage to cure scurvy. The addition of the pomegranate in this recipe is a fun twist on traditional mojito flavors. Like many drinks at Disney parks, this one comes and goes from La Cantina de San Angel's menu—but you can have it at home whenever you'd like!

SERVES 2

12 fresh mint leaves
2 ounces lime juice
2 ounces Simple Syrup (see recipe in Chapter 2)
10 ounces club soda
2 cups crushed ice
2 ounces Pomegranate Syrup (see recipe in Chapter 2)

1. Combine mint leaves, lime juice, and Simple Syrup in a cocktail shaker and muddle. Strain into a blender, discarding solids, and add club soda and ice. Blend until smooth.

2. Pour into two 16-ounce plastic cups or glasses and gently swirl 1 ounce Pomegranate Syrup into each glass.

Royal Blue

Oasis Sweets & Sips, EPCOT

* * * ✦ * * *

Though it's not one of the more popular beverages at Walt Disney World, the Royal Blue may just become a new favorite in your home. The yummy blend of blue raspberry and piña colada flavors creates a delicious combo perfect for a warm day. Even the color looks like a beautiful deep ocean. Grab your sunglasses and a towel, because this drink is about to transport you to paradise!

SERVES 1

8 ounces blue raspberry lemonade Kool-Aid Syrup (see recipe in Chapter 2)
2 ounces nonalcoholic piña colada mix
3 cups crushed ice

Add all ingredients to a blender and blend until smooth. Pour into a 20-ounce plastic cup or glass and serve immediately.

Shangri-La Berry Freeze

Warung Outpost, Disney's Animal Kingdom

* * * ✦ * * *

The fictional land of Shangri-La is a mythical paradise tucked into the Himalayan mountains—a utopia mere mortals could only wish to ascend to. This smoothie-like drink has a special combination of tart and sweet flavors sure to take your taste buds to nirvana! While sipping on this beverage in the Asia section of Disney's Animal Kingdom, it doesn't take much imagination to feel like you're in the real Shangri-La.

SERVES 1

3 cups frozen strawberries
½ cup nonalcoholic margarita mix
2 ounces Simple Syrup (see recipe in Chapter 2)
¼ cup lemonade

Add all ingredients to a blender and blend until smooth. Pour into a 16-ounce plastic cup or glass and serve immediately.

My Bugs! My Bugs!

Hollywood Lounge, Disney California Adventure

· · · ✳ · · ·

This drink is sold exclusively during Halloween time at the Disneyland Resort, including at the ticketed party Oogie Boogie Bash at Disney California Adventure. The sweet and sour flavors in the drink hearken to the inspiration for the drink itself: Oogie Boogie! This baddie from *The Nightmare Before Christmas* knows how to sweetly turn on the charm, as well as sour any relationship with his villainous behavior! Now you can enjoy his namesake beverage any time of the year right at home—just watch out for the (gummy) worms!

SERVES 1

6 ounces lemonade Kool-Aid Syrup (see recipe in Chapter 2)
2 ounces lime juice
3 cups crushed ice
1 ounce cherry syrup
4 gummy worms

Combine Kool-Aid Syrup, lime juice, and ice in a blender and blend until smooth. Pour into a 16-ounce plastic cup or glass and swirl in cherry syrup. Top with gummy worms.

DID YOU KNOW?

The woman who voiced Sally in The Nightmare Before Christmas *also played the mom, Kate, in* Home Alone: Catherine O'Hara! Both movies can be viewed on Disney+.

Night Blossom

Pongu Pongu, Disney's Animal Kingdom

· · · ✳ · · ·

The Night Blossom has quietly risen in the ranks to become one of the most beloved beverages in all of the Disney Parks. Guests make their way to the tiny window at Pongu Pongu in Pandora just to get one. Lines for the shop tend to get exceptionally long, and a designated Cast Member has to manage the queue with an "End of Line" sign, just like for a popular attraction. One nice thing about making this at home? No line! Strawberry watermelon juice can be found in the juice section of most grocery stores.

SERVES 2

2 cups limeade
½ cup frozen apple juice concentrate
1 cup strawberry watermelon juice
2 drops pink gel food coloring
1 drop purple gel food coloring
1 cup lime sherbet
¼ cup lemon-lime soda
½ cup passion fruit popping pearls, drained

1. Mix together limeade, apple juice concentrate, and strawberry watermelon juice in a pitcher or large mixing bowl. Pour mixture into an ice cream machine and run according to manufacturer's instructions 8 minutes or until slushy. Drop in pink and purple food coloring and run machine 1 more minute.

2. In a blender, blend together lime sherbet and lemon-lime soda.

3. Set aside half of the pink limeade mix, and divide the other half evenly into the bottoms of two tall drinking glasses. Divide green sherbet mix evenly and layer on top of the pink mix in the glasses, then layer on the remaining pink mix. Top with popping pearls and add large gauge straws.

Sleigh-Ride Slush

Hollywood Lounge, Disney California Adventure

. . . ✦ . . .

This seasonal offering may become one of your new holiday traditions. The unorthodox mix of lemonade, cranberry, and apple gives a tasty result with a markedly yuletide flair. Blend up a batch at your next holiday party and just wait for guests to ask how you made it.

SERVES 1

½ cup lemonade Kool-Aid Syrup (see recipe in Chapter 2)
½ cup cranberry-apple juice
3 cups crushed ice

Add all ingredients to a blender and blend until smooth. Pour into a 16-ounce plastic cup or glass and serve immediately.

Incredible Frozen Flame

Joffrey's Locations, Walt Disney World Resort

. . . ✦ . . .

The Incredible Frozen Flame is a seasonal offering sold at various Joffrey's locations around Walt Disney World Resort. Passion fruit and strawberry slushes are made separately and gently stirred together to retain their individual flavors as well as create a new combined flavor. Make it at home any time of year!

SERVES 1

4 ounces strawberry syrup
2 ounces club soda, divided
3 cups crushed ice, divided
4 ounces passion fruit syrup

1. Add strawberry syrup, 1 ounce club soda, and 1½ cups ice to a blender and blend until smooth. Pour into a 20-ounce plastic cup or glass. Rinse out blender.

2. Add passion fruit syrup, remaining 1 ounce club soda, and remaining 1½ cups ice to blender. Blend until smooth. Pour into glass and gently swirl.

Frozen Apple Cider

Backlot Express, Disney's Hollywood Studios

· · · ✦ · · ·

Halloween at the Walt Disney World Resort is one of the best times of year to visit. Just sampling the themed food and beverages is worth an October trip! This drink is refreshing (which you need because it's still hot in Orlando in October) and fun. The popping pearls give bright flavor to the drink. A spooky "poison apple" Disney glow cube is also served with this delicious offering when you buy it at the park. Use this recipe for a magical taste of Halloween any time of year.

SERVES 1

2 ounces Granny Smith apple syrup
4 ounces apple juice
2 cups crushed ice
¼ cup green apple popping pearls

Add apple syrup, apple juice, and ice to a blender. Blend until smooth. Pour into a 16-ounce plastic cup or glass and top with popping pearls.

Space Ranger Slushies

Auntie Gravity's Galactic Goodies, Magic Kingdom

. . . ✦ . . .

To infinity, and beyond! Hold on tight to your space laser, because this supersweet drink is going to ignite your rocket boosters! Sold at Auntie Gravity's in Tomorrowland at Magic Kingdom, this drink can be used as fuel right before taking on Emperor Zurg on Buzz Lightyear's Space Ranger Spin. If you'd like to re-create the experience at home, whip up a batch of these slushies and pop in a silly shooter video game the whole family can enjoy.

SERVES 2

For Slushies

4 ounces grape Kool-Aid Syrup (see recipe in Chapter 2)

2 ounces club soda, divided

3 cups crushed ice, divided

4 ounces green apple Kool-Aid Syrup (see recipe in Chapter 2)

For Candy-Coated Straws

6 green apple Jolly Rancher candies

6 green apple Life Savers candies, crushed

1. To make Slushies: Add grape Kool-Aid Syrup, 1 ounce club soda, and 1½ cups ice to a blender. Blend until smooth and pour into a medium bowl. Rinse blender and then add green apple Kool-Aid Syrup, remaining 1 ounce club soda, and remaining 1½ cups ice. Blend until smooth and pour into a separate medium bowl.

2. To make Candy-Coated Straws: Microwave Jolly Ranchers on high 1 minute in a small microwave-safe bowl. Pour crushed Life Savers into a shallow dish. Use a butter knife to smooth melted Jolly Ranchers three-quarters of the way up the length of a plastic straw, then quickly roll straw in Life Savers. Repeat with a second straw.

3. Layer slushy flavors in two tall plastic cups or glasses. Add Candy-Coated Straws (exposed side down) and serve immediately.

The American Dream

Fife & Drum Tavern, EPCOT

· · · ✦ · · ·

Could there be a more American food than this? Grab your stars and stripes, because this drink is invited to your next Fourth of July barbecue. Mixing the textures of soft serve and slush creates a party in your mouth. If you're enjoying this drink while at EPCOT, check the Times Guide to see when the Spirit of America Fife and Drum Corps are performing in the America Adventure Pavilion. They really stir feelings of the land of the free, home of the brave!

SERVES 1

2 ounces strawberry Kool-Aid Syrup (see recipe in Chapter 2)
1 ounce club soda, divided
2 cups crushed ice, divided
1 cup vanilla soft serve ice cream
2 ounces blue raspberry lemonade Kool-Aid Syrup (see recipe in Chapter 2)

1. Add strawberry Kool-Aid Syrup, ½ ounce club soda, and 1 cup ice to a blender and blend until smooth. Pour into a 20-ounce plastic cup or glass. Scoop ice cream on top. Rinse out blender.

2. Add blue raspberry Kool-Aid Syrup, remaining ½ ounce club soda, and remaining 1 cup ice to the blender and blend until smooth. Pour on top of ice cream. Serve immediately.

Wheezy's Breezy Freezy Frozen Coke

Hey Howdy Hey! Takeaway, Disney's Hollywood Studios

. . . ✦ . . .

Wheezy's Breezy Freezy actually comes in Coke, Wild Cherry, Lemonade, or Watermelon flavors. These positively fluffy drinks provide the sugar rush one needs when spending an afternoon in Toy Story Land. Being at home is no different. What afternoon couldn't benefit from a sweet pick-me-up? It may be just what you need to take on your bills, tackle that project you've been meaning to do, and finally grab that three-eyed alien in the arcade! This drink was served at Hey Howdy Hey! Takeaway during the opening of Toy Story Land, but the snack stand was later removed.

SERVES 1

20 ounces Coca-Cola, divided
1 ounce Simple Syrup (see recipe in Chapter 2)

Pour 12 ounces Coca-Cola into an ice cube tray and chill until frozen solid, about 6 hours or overnight. Remove cubes from tray and add to a blender with remaining 8 ounces Coca-Cola and Simple Syrup. Blend until smooth. Pour into a 20-ounce plastic cup or glass and serve immediately.

Sultan's Colada *(pictured)*

Oasis Sweets & Sips, EPCOT

· · · ✳ · · ·

This drink is similar to a typical piña colada, but the addition of pineapple juice after being blended creates a fun twist. Instead of being totally frozen, the liquid pineapple juice gives a refreshing touch. If you like your Dole Whip as a float, you'll definitely love this drink!

SERVES 1

6 ounces nonalcoholic piña colada mix
4 ounces cream of coconut
2 cups crushed ice
4 ounces pineapple juice

Combine piña colada mix, cream of coconut, and ice in a blender and blend until smooth. Pour into a 16-ounce plastic cup or glass and top with pineapple juice. Serve immediately.

Violet Lemonade

Pineapple Promenade, EPCOT

· · · ✳ · · ·

Did you know that violets themselves are edible? The blue or white varieties can be eaten, both the flower and the leaves, and contain high amounts of vitamins C and A. So don't worry about purchasing expensive specialty flowers for this recipe—you can go to your local garden store or flower shop! Of course, if eating flowers isn't your thing, omitting the flower is perfectly fine as well.

SERVES 1

5 ounces violet syrup
4 ounces lemonade
1 drop blue gel food coloring
1 drop red gel food coloring
3 cups crushed ice
1 edible violet flower

Add violet syrup, lemonade, food colorings, and ice to a blender and blend until smooth. Pour into a 20-ounce plastic cup or glass and top with edible flower.

Toydaria Swirl

Milk Stand, Disneyland

* * * ✳ * * *

Disneyland introduced this spin on the original Green Milk served in Star Wars: Galaxy's Edge as part of the second culinary rollout of the Land. Chamoy and chili-lime are Mexican seasonings, but they somehow feel at home in this drink. Be prepared for a spicy sip!

SERVES 2

½ cup rice milk
½ cup unsweetened canned coconut milk
1 cup pulp-free orange juice
1 cup passion fruit juice
¼ cup light corn syrup
3 drops lime-green gel food coloring
1 tablespoon chamoy sauce
1 teaspoon chili-lime seasoning blend

1. Add milks, orange juice, passion fruit juice, corn syrup, and food coloring to a blender and blend until smooth.

2. Pour mixture into an ice cream machine. Follow manufacturer's instructions and run about 10 minutes or until slushy.

3. Prepare two 12-ounce plastic cups or glasses by drizzling chamoy sauce evenly down the insides. Pour slushy mixture into prepared glasses and top with chili-lime seasoning. Enjoy immediately.

MIX IT UP

If you aren't accustomed to chamoy or chili-lime seasoning, try starting with smaller quantities of each and adding more until the flavor suits your palate.

Witch's Frozen Brew

Prince Eric's Village Market, Magic Kingdom

· · · ✦ · · ·

It seems like a wicked witch created this drink—one who had a real sweet tooth! But it also seems like someone at Prince Eric's Village Market just said, "Let's put every drink ingredient we have into one drink!" Either way, this recipe is sweet and strange. Be sure to give it a good stir before diving in, or you will be drinking pure syrup up the straw. The best part is the frozen Coca-Cola on top, which creates a look of a witch cauldron bubbling over! This drink is only available at Walt Disney World during the months of September and October, but with this recipe, you can enjoy it any time of year.

SERVES 1

8 ounces Coca-Cola, divided
½ ounce Simple Syrup (see recipe in Chapter 2)
4 ounces lemonade Kool-Aid Syrup (see recipe in Chapter 2)
1½ cups crushed ice
½ ounce cherry syrup
½ ounce Granny Smith apple syrup
½ ounce watermelon syrup
½ ounce red passion fruit syrup

1. Pour 4 ounces Coca-Cola into an ice cube tray and chill until frozen solid, about 6 hours or overnight. Remove cubes from tray and add to a blender with remaining 4 ounces Coca-Cola and Simple Syrup. Blend until smooth. Pour into a small cup or bowl. Rinse out blender.

2. Pour Kool-Aid Syrup into blender with ice. Blend until smooth. Pour into a separate small cup or bowl.

3. In a 20-ounce plastic cup or glass, add cherry, apple, watermelon, and passion fruit syrups. Pour lemonade slush on top of syrups. Pour Coca-Cola slush on top of lemonade slush. Serve immediately.

CHAPTER 5

Coffee, Tea, Hot Chocolate, & Cider

Sixty-two percent of Americans drink a cup of coffee every single day. This number may seem high, but that ranks the US as twenty-fifth in coffee drinkers across the world per capita. If you are a coffee drinker, why not give your caffeine routine a little more pizzazz by having a Disney-inspired drink in the morning? The recipes in this chapter have the power to put a smile on your face and start your day out on the right foot.

And have no fear: There is plenty here for the non–coffee drinker as well! See Chapter 2 to learn more about how to turn coffee drinks into non-coffee drinks with a simple ingredient swap. Also included in this chapter are tea, hot chocolate, and cider recipes sure to please even the youngest of your family members. Curl up with a good book by the fire and sip on a Hot Holiday Cider, or don your flight suit and lightsaber before trying the Orange Spice Black Spire Hot Chocolate. However you want to enjoy these drinks, make them yours, and have fun!

Black Spire Hot Chocolate

Docking Bay 7 Food and Cargo, Disneyland

· · · ✦ · · ·

Black Spire Outpost is home to some of the roughest thugs, smugglers, gangsters, and bounty hunters in the galaxy. But even ruffians like to kick off their boots on a cold winter's day and sip some hot chocolate with out-of-this-world purple whipped cream on top. The smooth hint of brown sugar in the chocolate, alongside the cream, will have your friends asking what your secret is. You can tell them, or play it close to the chest, because you're the mob boss of your own kitchen! Black Spire Hot Chocolate is a holiday offering at Disneyland, but can be whipped up in your kitchen any time of year.

SERVES 4

For Hot Chocolate

- 3½ cups whole milk
- ⅓ cup unsweetened cocoa powder
- 1 cup granulated sugar
- ⅛ teaspoon salt
- ⅓ cup water
- 1 teaspoon vanilla extract
- 4 tablespoons light brown sugar
- ½ cup half-and-half

For Brown Sugar Whipped Cream

- 6 ounces heavy whipping cream
- ¼ cup light brown sugar
- ⅛ teaspoon salt
- 1 teaspoon vanilla extract
- 2 drops purple gel food coloring

1. To make Hot Chocolate: In a medium saucepan over medium heat, combine milk, cocoa powder, granulated sugar, salt, water, vanilla, and brown sugar. Stir continuously until well mixed and hot, about 5–10 minutes. Pour into four large cups or mugs and add ⅛ cup half-and-half to each.

2. To make Brown Sugar Whipped Cream: Combine cream, brown sugar, and salt in the bowl of a stand mixer and beat until stiff peaks form, about 3–5 minutes. Mix in vanilla and food coloring until well combined. Pipe or scoop ¼ cup whipped cream onto each mug. Serve immediately.

Abuelita Hot Cocoa

¡Viva Navidad! Snack Cart, Disney California Adventure

· · · ✦ · · ·

Abuelita is actually a brand of Mexican hot chocolate that is sold in "pucks" you dissolve in hot milk. If you want the authentic experience, it can be purchased in the Mexican section at most grocery stores. This recipe re-creates the flavors of Mexican chocolate from scratch. Feel free to adjust the amount of each spice to make a custom blend that perfectly suits your taste. This hot drink can be found in November and December at Disney California Adventure.

SERVES 2

2 cups whole milk
2 tablespoons unsweetened cocoa powder
2 tablespoons bittersweet chocolate chips
1 tablespoon granulated sugar
¼ teaspoon ground cardamom
¼ teaspoon ground cinnamon
⅛ teaspoon cayenne pepper
¼ cup heavy whipping cream

1. Combine milk, cocoa powder, chocolate chips, sugar, cardamom, cinnamon, and cayenne in a small saucepan over medium heat. Cook, stirring continuously, until all ingredients are melted, combined, and hot, about 5–10 minutes.

2. Pour into two mugs. Top each with ⅛ cup whipped cream. Serve immediately.

Bubble Milk Tea

Joy of Tea, EPCOT

· · · ✦ · · ·

Bubble milk tea is a popular beverage in East and Southeast Asia and is growing in popularity throughout the US. Tapioca boba balls are labor intensive to make from scratch, so I recommend purchasing premade boba either online or at your local Asian market. If tapioca boba balls aren't to your liking, feel free to omit them from this recipe. They don't add much flavor to the tea—they just provide a chewy little snack in the bottom of your cup. Experiment with different tea flavors and see which you love best!

SERVES 1

½ cup hot water
1 peach tea bag (black or herbal)
1 tablespoon light brown sugar
¼ cup tapioca boba balls, cooked according to package instructions
1 cup ice cubes
½ cup half-and-half

1. Pour hot water into a mug and allow tea bag to steep 5 minutes. Squeeze bag into mug and then discard bag.

2. Add sugar to mug, stir to dissolve, and place mug in refrigerator to chill 10 minutes.

3. Add boba balls and ice to a 16-ounce plastic cup or glass. Pour in tea and half-and-half. Add a large gauge straw and enjoy immediately.

Espresso Gelato Affogato *(pictured)*

Gelato Stand, EPCOT

* * * ✦ * * *

Some people like their coffee hot. Some people like their coffee iced. But you're the kind of person who asks, "Why can't I have both?" Enjoy hot and cold coffee flavors by adding a scoop of ice cream to your cup of joe! This recipe is totally customizable. Sub espresso for coffee or a coffee substitute. Pick any flavor of ice cream you've got in the freezer. Use sugar cookies and wafer cookies, or don't! This is your *Expression* Gelato Affogato now.

SERVES 1

½ cup vanilla gelato
2 ounces hot espresso
2 small sugar cookies
1 cylindrical wafer cookie
1 tablespoon coffee beans

Scoop gelato into a small bowl. Pour hot espresso over gelato. Top with sugar cookies placed like Mickey ears and wafer cookie as a straw. Sprinkle coffee beans on top. Serve immediately.

French Vanilla Iced Coffee

Isle of Java, Disney's Animal Kingdom

* * * ✦ * * *

Isle of Java is located on Discovery Island, on the path that leads to DinoLand U.S.A. at Disney's Animal Kingdom. From this spot, you can catch some awesome entertainment, like the Hakuna Matata Time Dance Party. Join characters like Baloo, Terk, Koda, and more as you all rock out to the beat. If you are having this coffee at home, play *The Lion King* soundtrack to get that "Hakuna Matata" feeling in your own kitchen.

SERVES 1

1 cup ice cubes
1 cup hot coffee or coffee
   substitute, chilled
½ cup French vanilla liquid
   coffee creamer

Add ice to a 16-ounce plastic cup or glass and pour in chilled coffee or coffee substitute and creamer. Stir to combine. Serve immediately.

Cinderella Latte

Starbucks Locations, Walt Disney World Resort and Disneyland Resort

· · · ✦ · · ·

This drink is not an official Walt Disney World beverage. It isn't even an official Starbucks beverage! Like many of the cute, themed drinks served at Starbucks, this is from the "secret menu," a fan-created list of recipes tweaked to fit a certain look or flavor. This drink can be ordered at any Starbucks, using the specifications below. But why spend good money when you can make it just as well at home?

SERVES 1

4 ounces strong coffee or coffee substitute
1 ounce pumpkin pie spice syrup
1 ounce white chocolate syrup
4 ounces cold whole milk
½ cup ice cubes
¼ cup whipped cream
⅛ teaspoon clear sprinkles

1. Combine coffee or coffee substitute with pumpkin pie spice syrup and white chocolate syrup in a 16-ounce plastic cup or glass.

2. Add milk and ice to glass. Top with whipped cream and sprinkles.

Pumpkin Pie Latte

Joffrey's Locations, Walt Disney World Resort

· · · ✦ · · ·

The pumpkin spice latte, or "PSL," is an iconic drink of fall. Available during the cooler months, the Pumpkin Pie Latte is Joffrey's take on the PSL. Don your sweater and boots because this drink is autumn in a cup! Feel free to substitute the espresso for black coffee, coffee substitute, hot chocolate, or even milk.

SERVES 1

2 ounces espresso
1 ounce pumpkin pie spice syrup
8 ounces steamed whole milk

Combine espresso, pumpkin pie spice syrup, and milk in an insulated cup or mug. Enjoy immediately.

Toffee Flight Hot Chocolate

Joffrey's Locations, Walt Disney World Resort

· · · ✦ · · ·

This specialty drink was made to be sold at Joffrey's locations situated outside the Skyliner stations at Walt Disney World. You can order it as a hot chocolate, hot latte, or iced latte! Disney's Skyliner opened in fall 2019, providing a speedy (and fun!) way to get from point A to point B. Disney's Art of Animation, Pop Century, Caribbean Beach, and Riviera resorts all have stations that take guests to Disney's Hollywood Studios and EPCOT. Enjoy this drink during your morning commute from point A to point B.

SERVES 1

1 (1.38-ounce) packet hot chocolate mix
6 ounces hot water
2 ounces sea salt caramel sauce, divided
1 ounce dark chocolate sauce
¼ cup steamed whole milk
¼ cup whipped cream
1 tablespoon toffee bits

Combine hot chocolate mix, water, 1½ ounces caramel sauce, chocolate sauce, and milk in an insulated cup or mug. Top with whipped cream, drizzle with remaining ½ ounce caramel sauce, and sprinkle with toffee bits.

Hot Chocolate Affogato

Vivoli il Gelato, Disney Springs

. . . ✦ . . .

This recipe creates hot chocolate from scratch, but if you're looking for a quicker and easier solution, feel free to use your favorite premade hot chocolate packet. You can buy whatever flavor packet you love, like caramel sea salt or French vanilla. If you are looking for a more involved recipe, make the vanilla ice cream from scratch! However you decide to enjoy it, rich hot chocolate and creamy cold ice cream fuse together for the perfect treat any time of year.

SERVES 4

2 cups whole milk
½ cup milk chocolate chips
½ cup semisweet chocolate chips
2 tablespoons unsweetened cocoa powder
⅛ teaspoon salt
2 cups vanilla ice cream, divided
1 cup canned whipped cream

1. Combine milk, all chocolate chips, cocoa powder, and salt in a medium saucepan over medium heat. Cook about 10 minutes or until all ingredients are melted and well combined.

2. Divide ice cream into four mugs. Pour hot chocolate over ice cream, top with whipped cream, and serve immediately.

Hot Holiday Cider

Refreshment Cart, Magic Kingdom

* * * ✦ * * *

This Hot Holiday Cider is served seasonally at a cart in the Magic Kingdom hub right in front of Cinderella Castle. What may appear to be a typical cider is elevated by the gingerbread syrup. Disney Parks undergo an incredible transformation on November 1 each year, most of which takes place in the predawn hours. All the Halloween decorations disappear and are replaced with jingle bells, wreaths, and ribbons! Can you imagine the size of the team required to pull off this magic??

SERVES 6

8 large Granny Smith apples, cored and quartered
1 tablespoon ground cinnamon
1 tablespoon ground allspice
1 cup granulated sugar
10 cups water
3 ounces gingerbread syrup

1. Add apples, cinnamon, allspice, sugar, and water to an 8-quart slow cooker. Stir to combine and secure lid. Cook on high 4 hours.

2. Mash slow cooker contents with a potato masher or whisk, then carefully strain into a pitcher, discarding solids. To get a finer consistency, re-strain cider through a cloth.

3. Pour hot cider into six mugs and add ½ ounce gingerbread syrup to each mug. Stir well. Serve immediately or chilled. Leftovers can be refrigerated up to 5 days and reheated on a stovetop over medium-high heat.

Hot Spiced Apple Cider

Lobby, Disney's Grand Californian Hotel & Spa

· · · · ✦ · · ·

Nothing could be cozier than a stay at Disney's Grand Californian Hotel & Spa during holiday time. This hotel is designed after the Arts and Crafts movement of California in the early 1900s. Rustic luxury abounds during the holiday season and includes a massive gingerbread house assembled right in the lobby. Whether or not your home can be described as "rustic luxury," having a Hot Spiced Apple Cider in your PJs sure sounds mighty cozy! This drink is a seasonal offering at Disney's Grand Californian Hotel & Spa.

SERVES 6

8 large Granny Smith apples, cored and quartered
1 tablespoon ground cinnamon
1 tablespoon ground allspice
1 cup granulated sugar
10 cups water
3 ounces vanilla syrup
6 cinnamon sticks

1. Add apples, cinnamon, allspice, sugar, and water to an 8-quart slow cooker. Stir to combine and cover. Cook on high 4 hours.

2. Mash contents in slow cooker with a potato masher or whisk, then carefully pour through a strainer into a pitcher and discard solids. To get a finer consistency, pour strained liquid through a cloth.

3. Pour cider into six mugs and add ½ ounce vanilla syrup to each mug. Stir well. Garnish each mug with a cinnamon stick.

4. Serve immediately or chilled. Leftovers can be covered and chilled up to 5 days. Reheat on stovetop over medium-high heat.

Teddy's Tea *(pictured)*

Jock Lindsey's Hangar Bar, Disney Springs

· · · ✦ · · ·

Jock Lindsey from *Indiana Jones and the Raiders of the Lost Ark* was played by Fred Sorenson. The bar is obviously based off of the fictional character, Jock, but is also about Fred. If you take a look to the right side of the bar, there is a painting of a man in a Yankees baseball hat: This is Fred Sorenson! He was an avid traveler himself and took exotic adventures just like Jock did. Jock would probably stop in for a Teddy's Tea if he could, and delight in the fresh pops of mint and tangerine.

SERVES 1

8 ounces cold green tea
1 small tangerine,
   quartered
1 cup ice cubes
1 sprig fresh mint

Pour green tea into a regular drinking glass. Squeeze juice from tangerine slices into tea and drop spent slices into glass. Top with ice and garnish with mint sprig.

Frozen Cappuccinos

Joffrey's Locations, Walt Disney World Resort

· · · ✦ · · ·

This recipe takes iced coffee to the next level by blending it to a smooth, slushy consistency. This offering comes and goes at Walt Disney World, where you can actually get an image of Mickey printed onto the top of your Frozen Cappuccino. You probably don't have a coffee printer at home, but I promise this will taste just as good without it!

SERVES 2

1½ cups coffee or coffee
   substitute, chilled
½ cup French vanilla liquid
   coffee creamer
1 tablespoon Simple Syrup
   (see recipe in Chapter 2)
2 cups crushed ice

Add all ingredients to a blender and blend until smooth. Pour into two 16-ounce plastic cups or glasses and serve immediately.

Winter Hot Chocolate

Hollywood Lounge, Disney California Adventure

. . . ✦ . . .

Nothing says holiday time quite like peppermint, and this seasonal drink has peppermint flavor in spades. The peppermint extract in the cocoa and crushed candy cane sprinkled on top make for a cooling zip that feels great in contrast to the hot liquid. A Disney glow cube of Mickey is served with this festive drink in the park, but instead you could garnish with a whole candy cane to act as a stir stick.

SERVES 4

3½ cups whole milk
⅓ cup unsweetened cocoa powder
1 cup granulated sugar
⅛ teaspoon salt
⅓ cup water
1 teaspoon peppermint extract
½ cup half-and-half
2 cups whipped cream, divided
1 candy cane, crushed

1. Combine milk, cocoa powder, sugar, salt, and water in a medium saucepan over medium heat. Stir continuously until well mixed and hot, about 3–5 minutes. Remove from heat and stir in peppermint extract.

2. Pour into four mugs. Top each mug with ⅛ cup half-and-half and a swirl of whipped cream. Sprinkle on crushed candy cane pieces. Serve immediately.

Toasted Marshmallow–Flavored Hot Cocoa

Wandering Oaken's Trading Post, Disney's Hollywood Studios

· · · ✦ · · ·

This delicious holiday treat was served for only a few years at Disney's Hollywood Studios while Wandering Oaken's Trading Post was open. It hasn't been available since 2015. But with the magic of this homemade recipe, you can have it anytime! Although it seems like a typical cup of cocoa, the addition of toasted marshmallow syrup lends a rich, creamy flavor unique to this drink. Big summer blowout!

SERVES 4

3½ cups whole milk
⅓ cup unsweetened cocoa powder
1 cup granulated sugar
⅛ teaspoon salt
⅓ cup water
1 teaspoon vanilla extract
4 ounces toasted marshmallow syrup
½ cup half-and-half
2 cups whipped cream

1. Combine milk, cocoa powder, sugar, salt, and water in a medium saucepan over medium heat. Stir continuously until well mixed and hot, about 3–5 minutes. Remove from heat and stir in vanilla and toasted marshmallow syrup.

2. Pour into four mugs. Top each mug with ⅛ cup half-and-half and a swirl of whipped cream. Serve immediately.

DID YOU KNOW?

The ending of Frozen II *was changed several times before the final film came out. Up until a few months before release, it wasn't decided whom Elsa would encounter once she reached Ahtohallan!*

CHAPTER 6

Mocktails

We've visited a lot of mixed drinks in this book, yet here we are at a chapter called Mocktails. What *is* a mocktail? What sets it apart from any other mixed drink? The first thing is the lack of alcohol. Unlike cocktails, mocktails don't contain any alcohol and are therefore accessible to every member of the family. Secondly, mocktails typically are not slushes or daiquiris: They are usually a cold drink served with ice. And lastly, a mocktail is a mocktail because of *where* the drink is served. They are usually served at a bar or lounge alongside mixed alcoholic beverages.

In this chapter, you'll explore some of Disney's most popular mocktails, from the out-of-this-world Blue Bantha and Blurrgfire to the beloved New Orleans Mint Julep and Sparkling No-Jito. Go forth and enjoy these teetotaler treats!

Blue Bantha

Oga's Cantina, Disneyland and Disney's Hollywood Studios

· · · ✦ · · ·

When you order this item at Oga's Cantina, you get a beverage *and* a snack! A huge, caramelly, buttery, coconutty cookie is perched on top of a glass of chilled Blue Milk. The "milk" is said to have been extracted from banthas, a beast of burden found on Tatooine and Batuu. Tusken Raiders ride them in single file to disguise their numbers. Luke Skywalker's aunt Beru served blue bantha milk with meals at her table. You can do the same!

SERVES 4

For Bantha Cookies

- 4 large egg whites
- ½ teaspoon cream of tartar
- ¼ teaspoon plus ⅛ teaspoon salt, divided
- 2 cups granulated sugar, divided
- 1 tablespoon plus 1 teaspoon vanilla extract, divided
- 1 cup salted butter, softened
- 1 large egg
- 2 tablespoons heavy whipping cream
- 2½ cups all-purpose flour
- 1 teaspoon baking powder

1. The Bantha Cookies and Coconut Caramel will be made in three parts and assembled after baking. To make the meringue horn part of Bantha Cookies, preheat oven to 225°F and line a baking sheet with parchment paper.

2. Combine egg whites, cream of tartar, and ⅛ teaspoon salt in the bowl of a stand mixer. Using whisk attachment, whisk until mixture becomes foamy, about 3–5 minutes. Slowly add in 1 cup sugar, 1 spoonful at a time while whisking, until mixture is shiny and thick, and stiff peaks have formed. Add in 1 teaspoon vanilla and whisk to combine.

3. Scoop meringue into a piping bag fitted with a small round tip. Pipe twelve crescent-shaped "horns," about 3" in diameter, onto the prepared baking sheet. Bake 1 hour until dry and stiff. Remove pan from oven and set aside. Extra horns can be stored in an airtight container at room temperature up to 3 days.

(continued) ▶

Diving Bell *(pictured)*

Jock Lindsey's Hangar Bar, Disney Springs

· · · ✦ · · ·

Although simple, this drink is a fun diversion from classic lemonade. Leaving the watermelon syrup on the bottom of the glass creates an ombré effect that makes for a gorgeous presentation! Jock Lindsey's Hangar Bar at Disney Springs is an homage to the fictional pilot from *Indiana Jones and the Raiders of the Lost Ark*. The walls and ceiling are covered with memorabilia from Jock's travels. Next time you're there, take a look around and see how many nods to the Indiana Jones franchise you can find.

SERVES 1

1 cup ice cubes
1½ ounces watermelon syrup
8 ounces lemonade
2 lemon wheels

Fill a regular drinking glass with ice. Add watermelon syrup, then lemonade. Garnish with lemon wheels on either side of the glass to look like Mickey ears. Insert a straw and serve.

Zingiber Fizzie

Nomad Lounge, Disney's Animal Kingdom

· · · ✦ · · ·

If you get a chance to visit Nomad Lounge while at Disney's Animal Kingdom, do it! It is attached to the superpopular restaurant Tiffins, but no reservation is required at the lounge. Munch on some small bites and sip on inventive drinks like this one. The ginger beer gives a little fizz to cool you down on a hot day.

SERVES 1

2 ounces passion fruit juice
1 ounce Simple Syrup (see recipe in Chapter 2)
½ ounce lime juice
3 fresh mint leaves
5 ounces ginger beer
1 sprig mint

Combine passion fruit juice, Simple Syrup, lime juice, and mint leaves in a regular drinking glass and muddle. Add ice to nearly fill, then top with ginger beer. Garnish with mint sprig.

Cliff Dweller

Oga's Cantina, Disneyland and Disney's Hollywood Studios

· · · ✦ · · ·

Most of the nonalcoholic drinks at Oga's are in the $6–$8 range, so seeing the Cliff Dweller at $35 might come as a shock! But this is a beverage and souvenir all in one, as it comes with a porg mug you get to take home with you. Souvenirs like this are great because you can see them in your kitchen and use them more frequently than some other trinkets you might pick up. You can serve this drink up in your porg mug if you have one! Porg mug or not, the Cliff Dweller is delicious and fruity, with an unexpected twist of hibiscus syrup. If you don't have hibiscus syrup, try subbing it out for a syrup flavor you do have, like cherry, strawberry, or Simple Syrup (see recipe in Chapter 2).

SERVES 1

3 ounces pulp-free orange juice
3 ounces pineapple juice
1 ounce lime juice
½ ounce hibiscus syrup
1 ounce ginger ale
1 ounce cream of coconut

Add all ingredients to a cocktail shaker half full of ice, seal, and shake well. Pour into a regular drinking glass and fill with ice.

DID YOU KNOW?

When DJ R3X plays the song "Una Duey Dee," locals of Batuu know this is a song for chanting. If you are in the bar when the song comes on, raise your glass and yell, "Hey!" to the tune!

Hoodunit's Punch

AbracadaBar, Disney's BoardWalk

· · · ✦ · · ·

The bright flavors of this tropical drink are sure to leave you smiling. A delicious combination of fruit juices and coconut, offset by the tart cranberry juice, provides an escape from the ordinary. You'll love the layered effect created by adding the cranberry juice last—it's sure to impress your friends and family! This drink is also offered at AbracadaBar with rum.

SERVES 1

6 ounces pineapple juice
2 ounces pulp-free orange juice
1 ounce cream of coconut
1 cup ice cubes
2 ounces cranberry juice
1 pineapple wedge
1 maraschino cherry

Add pineapple juice, orange juice, and cream of coconut to a cocktail shaker half full of ice. Seal and shake well, then pour into a regular drinking glass. Add ice cubes and top with cranberry juice without stirring. Garnish with pineapple wedge and maraschino cherry on a toothpick.

DID YOU KNOW?

Next time you visit AbracadaBar at Disney's BoardWalk, ask to see the famous AbraLadder. It's literally a stepladder that Disney fans have decided is important. It has its own plaque and hundreds of hashtag posts!

Hibiscus Henna *(pictured)*

Nomad Lounge, Disney's Animal Kingdom

· · · ✦ · · ·

A henna tattoo is a nonpermanent body marking that stays on for several days and then fades away. It is a less intense version of a real tattoo and is used in cultural and religious traditions in many countries around the world. The Hibiscus Henna drink is just like the Jenn's Tattoo drink also served at Nomad Lounge, but it doesn't contain alcohol. It is a less intense version of Jenn's Tattoo! Creative naming like this can be found across Disney properties, especially if you take the time to ask Cast Members for some stories.

SERVES 1

6 ounces club soda
1 ounce watermelon syrup
1 ounce hibiscus syrup
½ ounce lime juice
1 cup ice cubes
1 lime wheel

Combine club soda, watermelon syrup, hibiscus syrup, and lime juice in a regular drinking glass. Fill with ice and garnish with lime wheel.

Ghoulish Delight

Hollywood Lounge, Disney California Adventure

· · · ✦ · · ·

This Halloween offering is inspired by the spooky intro to the Haunted Mansion ride, but there's nothing creepy about this drink. It's all delight! Cotton candy is a fun and whimsical addition. If you don't have your own cotton candy machine, most grocery stores sell the stuff in the candy aisle.

SERVES 1

8 ounces lemonade
1 ounce cotton candy syrup
½ cup cotton candy

Combine lemonade and cotton candy syrup in a cocktail shaker half full of ice, seal, and shake well. Pour into a 16-ounce plastic cup or glass and top with ice until nearly full. Garnish with cotton candy.

Jabba Juice

Oga's Cantina, Disneyland and Disney's Hollywood Studios

· · · ✦ · · ·

This drink may just become your new favorite brunch beverage. The fruity juice flavors mixed with the surprising kiwi and cantaloupe syrups provide a delightful twist on classic orange juice. Jabba the Hutt features heavily (pun intended) in *Star Wars: Return of the Jedi* as a notorious gangster who terrorizes the galaxy with his access to a rancor and the Sarlacc. After his (spoiler alert) demise, Oga's Cantina must have named this drink in his honor.

SERVES 1

4 ounces pulp-free orange juice
2 ounces pineapple juice
1 ounce kiwi syrup
½ ounce rock melon cantaloupe syrup
¼ cup blueberry popping pearls

Add orange juice, pineapple juice, kiwi syrup, and cantaloupe syrup to a cocktail shaker half full of ice, seal, and shake well. Pour into a tall, skinny drinking glass and fill with ice. Add popping pearls on top.

Kiama Mamma

Nomad Lounge, Disney's Animal Kingdom

· · · ✦ · · ·

This drink may seem basic at first, but it's a twist on the classic Shirley Temple that may become a new favorite in your home. The refreshing flavor of watermelon paired with the fizzy lemon-lime soda makes for the perfect summer drink. Garnish with a watermelon wedge to elevate this drink to poolside royalty!

SERVES 1

8 ounces lemon-lime soda
1½ ounces watermelon syrup
1 watermelon wedge
1 cup ice cubes

Stir together lemon-lime soda and watermelon syrup in a regular drinking glass and fill with ice. Garnish with watermelon wedge.

Punch Line Punch

Jungle Navigation Co. LTD Skipper Canteen, Magic Kingdom

· · · ✦ · · ·

Jungle Navigation Co. LTD Skipper Canteen is the fictional hangout spot for Jungle Cruise skippers and intrepid explorers. Mango, passion fruit, and orange flavors provide even the most exhausted adventurers with a burst of fruity flavor sure to put a pep in their step! Be sure to check out the butterfly collection in the library next time you visit the canteen, and try a bite of the whole fried fish (it's almost certainly, definitely, probably not piranha!).

SERVES 1

6 ounces mango nectar
2 ounces passion fruit juice
2 ounces pulp-free orange juice
1 cup ice cubes

Add mango nectar, passion fruit juice, and orange juice to a regular drinking glass. Stir to combine. Top with ice.

MIXING TIP

Instead of using mango nectar, try peeling and cutting whole mangoes, blending them, and pouring the purée through a sieve. This will create a brighter, fresher flavor than a canned nectar.

Hyperdrive (Punch It!)

Oga's Cantina, Disneyland and Disney's Hollywood Studios

· · · ✦ · · ·

The iconic line "Punch it!" is first uttered by Han Solo in *Star Wars: The Empire Strikes Back*. This two-word exclamation is now one of the most recognizable lines in cinema. Similarly, this recipe is for one of the most recognizable drinks at Oga's Cantina, with an eye-catching blue-and-white blend and spacey-looking red ooze dripping between the ice. The unexpected "punch" in this drink is the black cherry purée, which makes it shine with a pop of flavor! The Hyperdrive (Punch It!) is nonalcoholic, so it's the perfect refreshment for the younger smugglers and bounty hunters in your crew.

SERVES 2

½ cup granulated sugar
½ cup pitted and quartered black cherries
1 tablespoon lemon juice
3 cups crushed ice
1 cup lemon-lime soda
½ cup white cranberry juice
1 cup Mountain Berry Blast Powerade

1. In a small saucepan over medium heat, combine sugar, black cherries, and lemon juice. Bring to a boil, then remove from heat.

2. Using an immersion blender or regular blender, purée cherry mixture. Texture should be like a soupy jam. Cover and chill at least 1 hour up to overnight.

3. When ready to assemble, divide ice evenly into two tall drinking glasses. Add ingredients split evenly into each glass in this order: lemon-lime soda, white cranberry juice, and Powerade. Do not stir!

4. Scoop 1 tablespoon black cherry purée gently onto top of ice in each glass. Serve immediately.

New Orleans Mint Julep *(pictured)*

Mint Julep Bar, Disneyland

. . . ✦ . . .

Mint juleps have been a Disneyland staple for years, with the original version going heavy on the mint and including buckets of green food coloring. Guests described the drink as tasting like mouthwash or toothpaste, so in 2017, the recipe was changed for a more natural flavor and lighter color. Guests loved it and continue to line up at the bar for New Orleans Mint Juleps!

SERVES 1

½ cup lemonade
½ cup club soda
2 tablespoons Mint Syrup
  (see recipe in Chapter 2)
1 cup ice cubes
1 lemon wheel
1 fresh mint leaf

Pour lemonade, club soda, and Mint Syrup into a 16-ounce plastic cup or glass. Stir to combine. Top with ice. Place lemon wheel on rim and mint leaf on ice to garnish.

Poisonless Dart

Jock Lindsey's Hangar Bar, Disney Springs

. . . ✦ . . .

Indiana Jones movies are fraught with all sorts of iconic weaponry, from Indy's whip and pistol to sabers and more. But the poison darts that greet audiences at the beginning of *Indiana Jones and the Raiders of the Lost Ark* certainly had a powerful impact. I know I wouldn't want to be in the middle of that melee! This Poisonless Dart is so named because it is alcohol-free and thus has no "sting."

SERVES 1

6 fresh mint leaves
1 ounce lime juice
1 ounce Simple Syrup (see
  recipe in Chapter 2)
1 cup ice cubes
6 ounces club soda
2 lime wheels

Combine mint leaves, lime juice, and Simple Syrup in a tall, skinny drinking glass and muddle together. Add ice and top with club soda. Add lime wheels to sides of glass to mimic Mickey ears.

Polynesian Punch

Trader Sam's Tiki Terrace, Disney's Polynesian Village Resort

· · · ✦ · · ·

Usually served in a plastic tiki tumbler with a bendy straw, this drink immediately evokes the spirit of the islands. Tiki tumblers are actually not hard to obtain and can be ordered from online retailers or even found in party supply stores. Although a fun, themed cup is not required to enjoy this drink, it sure helps to solidify the tropical feel. These bold, fresh flavors will surely transport you straight to the luau!

SERVES 1

2 ounces passion fruit juice
1 ounce pulp-free orange juice
1 ounce pineapple juice
½ ounce lemon juice
1 ounce guava nectar
½ ounce Orgeat (see recipe in Chapter 2)
½ ounce Falernum (see recipe in Chapter 2)
½ ounce Monin hibiscus syrup
1 cup ice cubes

Combine fruit juices, guava nectar, Orgeat, Falernum, and hibiscus syrup in a cocktail shaker half full of ice, seal, and shake well. Add ice to a regular drinking glass or tiki tumbler and pour juice over ice.

Skipper Sipper

Trader Sam's Tiki Terrace, Disney's Polynesian Village Resort

* * * ✳ * * *

When you top this drink with club soda, it creates a "sunset" effect that is just gorgeous. And it is as yummy as it is pretty. Falernum is a common tiki drink additive that lends a spiced, nutty flavor. Although this drink can be made without the Falernum, it really adds a wow factor that will have your friends and family guessing what makes the Skipper Sipper so special!

SERVES 1

8 fresh mint leaves, divided
1 ounce lime juice
½ ounce Agave Syrup (see recipe in Chapter 2)
½ ounce Falernum (see recipe in Chapter 2)
6 ounces pineapple-orange juice
1 cup ice cubes
2 ounces club soda

Combine 6 mint leaves, lime juice, Agave Syrup, Falernum, and pineapple-orange juice in a regular drinking glass and muddle. Add ice and top with club soda. Garnish with remaining 2 mint leaves.

Schweitzer Falls

Trader Sam's Tiki Terrace, Disney's Polynesian Village Resort

· · · · ✦ · · ·

The infamous Schweitzer Falls, named after the fictitious explorer Albert Falls, can be seen on the world-famous Jungle Cruise at both Disneyland and Magic Kingdom. The rock around the falls is limestone, but a lot of people take it for granite. When you ride the Jungle Cruise, don't forget to snap a picture of the highlight attraction—the backside of water—otherwise known as O_2H. Drinking this flavorful mocktail will have you regaling your friends and family with stories of the jungle!

SERVES 1

1 ounce passion fruit juice
1 ounce pulp-free orange juice
1 ounce pineapple juice
½ ounce lemon juice
1 ounce guava nectar
½ ounce Orgeat (see recipe in Chapter 2)
½ ounce Falernum (see recipe in Chapter 2)
1 cup ice cubes
2 ounces lemon-lime soda
1 maraschino cherry
1 pineapple leaf
1 pineapple wedge

1. Combine fruit juices, guava nectar, Orgeat, and Falernum in a cocktail shaker half full of ice, seal, and shake well. Add ice to a regular drinking glass and pour juice over ice. Top with lemon-lime soda.

2. Skewer maraschino cherry and pineapple leaf onto a toothpick and drive into pineapple wedge. Slit pineapple wedge and place on edge of glass. Top with a drink umbrella and serve.

Sparkling No-Jito *(pictured)*

Tambu Lounge, Disney's Polynesian Village Resort

· · · ✦ · · ·

This drink has flavors of lime and mint, like a mojito, but omits the alcohol—hence the "no"-jito name. Bartenders at Tambu Lounge create their mocktails and cocktails right at the bar for you to see. Next time you're there, request a seat at the bar, and you may learn a thing or two about drink mixing!

SERVES 1

2 ounces lime juice
1½ ounces Simple Syrup
(see recipe in Chapter 2)
8 fresh mint leaves, divided
1 cup ice cubes
8 ounces club soda

Add lime juice, Simple Syrup, and 6 mint leaves to a regular drinking glass and muddle. Add ice and top with club soda. Garnish with remaining 2 mint leaves.

Tropical Paradise

Banana Cabana, Disney's Caribbean Beach Resort

· · · ✦ · · ·

The alcoholic version of this drink is called a "painkiller," since some people try to take away the pain of a long night of drinking with one. However, a traditional painkiller includes rum, so does it really get the job done? This painkiller comes alcohol-free, so you can enjoy it anytime—without the hangover!

SERVES 1

4 ounces pineapple juice
1 ounce cream of coconut
2 ounces pulp-free orange
juice
½ ounce lime juice
⅛ teaspoon ground
cinnamon
⅛ teaspoon ground nutmeg

Add pineapple juice, cream of coconut, orange juice, lime juice, and cinnamon to a cocktail shaker half full of ice. Seal and shake well, then pour into a 16-ounce plastic cup or glass. Fill with ice and sprinkle nutmeg on top.

The Peachcomber

Banana Cabana, Disney's Caribbean Beach Resort

. . . ✳ . . .

Peach juice in a bottle can sometimes be hard to come by. If you have trouble locating some, mix 2 ounces peach syrup from a can of peaches with 2 ounces cold water. Add that to this beverage instead! Banana Cabana is a delightful poolside bar at Disney's Caribbean Beach Resort. Patrons can hold a Peachcomber while watching little buccaneers careen down the waterslide to protect the fort from pirates!

SERVES 1

2 ounces pulp-free
orange juice
2 ounces lemonade
4 ounces peach juice
2 ounces club soda

Add orange juice, lemonade, and peach juice to a cocktail shaker half full of ice, seal, and shake well. Pour into a 16-ounce plastic cup or glass and add ice almost to the brim. Pour club soda over ice.

Virgin Magic Mirror

AbracadaBar, Disney's BoardWalk

* * * ✦ * * *

When you order the Magic Mirror at AbracadaBar, ask the bartender to make it in front of you. The coloring is added at the end of the process and quickly changes the drink from light to dark purple! When you make this for party guests, be sure to do it with flair. Abracadabra!

½ ounce lime juice
1 ounce violet syrup
4 ounces club soda
4 ounces lemon-lime soda
½ ounce Simple Syrup (see recipe in Chapter 2)
3 drops purple gel food coloring
1 cup ice cubes
1 lime wheel

Combine lime juice, violet syrup, club soda, and lemon-lime soda in a tall, skinny drinking glass. Combine Simple Syrup and food coloring in a separate small cup, then add to glass. Fill with ice and garnish with lime wheel.

DID YOU KNOW?

At AbracadaBar, look for a newspaper article on the wall from the BoardWalk Bugle. It states that a group of illusionists and entertainers vanished into thin air at that spot on November 13, 1940. How mysterious!

CHAPTER 7

Cocktails

As you learned earlier in this book, cocktails and alcoholic drinks in general were not permitted at Disneyland or Magic Kingdom when they opened. However, adult beverages have been a part of every other Disney property beginning with the opening of EPCOT in 1982. Magic Kingdom started selling alcohol in 2012, and Disneyland in 2019. Disney Parks were created for family-friendly fun, but executives realized it isn't just the kids who need pleasing—the paying adults want to have fun too!

Now delicious and inventive cocktails are available across Disney Parks. Enjoy mixing these concoctions in your own home, Cast Member costume optional! And if you are a teetotaler like me, there are plenty of replacements for the alcoholic ingredients in this chapter. Feel free to experiment with these recipes and make them your own!

Dagobah Slug Slinger *(pictured)*

Oga's Cantina, Disneyland and Disney's Hollywood Studios

· · · · ✦ · · · ·

Rosemary and orange flavors provide an herbal, fruity experience while drinking this unique beverage from Star Wars: Galaxy's Edge. It's named for the swamp planet where Yoda trained Luke Skywalker in the Force.

SERVES 1

1 ounce reposado tequila
1 ounce Ginger Rosemary Simple Syrup (see recipe in Chapter 2)
¼ ounce lemon juice
¼ ounce lime juice
⅛ ounce blue curaçao
⅛ teaspoon orange bitters
1 small sprig fresh rosemary

Shake all ingredients except rosemary sprig in a sealed cocktail shaker filled with ice. Strain into a tiki glass filled with ice. Garnish with rosemary sprig.

Bespin Fizz

Oga's Cantina, Disneyland and Disney's Hollywood Studios

· · · · ✦ · · · ·

Bespin is a gas giant planet from the Star Wars universe and is known for its toxic clouds. Humans live in an upper layer of the atmosphere known as the "Life Zone." The Bespin Fizz plays on this concept by including a "cloud swirl," created with dry ice. For this cloudlike effect (and more texture) at home, add 1 egg white to the shaker!

SERVES 1

1 ounce white rum
¾ ounce yuzu purée
½ ounce white cranberry juice
½ ounce Simple Syrup (see recipe in Chapter 2)
¼ ounce pomegranate juice
1 teaspoon fondant glitter powder

1. Add all ingredients to a cocktail shaker with 1 ice cube. Seal and shake until you can't hear the ice anymore.

2. Add more ice, seal, and shake again, then strain into a martini glass.

Grapefruit Cake Martini

The Hollywood Brown Derby, Disney's Hollywood Studios

· · · ✦ · · ·

Few drinks are as inventive as this one. Grapefruit Cake was made popular by the original Brown Derby restaurant in Los Angeles, California, in the early 1900s. Created by the restaurant's chef and owner, Robert Cobb (who is also credited with creating the Cobb salad), this sweet and tart treat drew crowds. In homage to this creation, the Hollywood Brown Derby restaurant in Disney's Hollywood Studios serves this Grapefruit Cake Martini that has all the flavors of the original cake!

SERVES 1

1 graham cracker, crushed
1 fresh grapefruit wheel
1 ounce vanilla vodka
1 ounce grapefruit vodka
¾ ounce heavy whipping cream
¾ ounce Simple Syrup (see recipe in Chapter 2)
1 dehydrated grapefruit wheel

1. Pour graham cracker crumbs onto a small plate. Push a martini glass, rim down, on fresh grapefruit wheel to express juices and coat rim. Dip glass in crushed cracker and twist to coat rim with crumbs.

2. Shake all remaining ingredients except dehydrated grapefruit wheel in a sealed cocktail shaker filled with ice. Strain into a rimmed glass. Garnish with dehydrated grapefruit wheel.

Canadian Apple Slushy

The Daily Poutine, Disney Springs

. . . ✦ . . .

Appearing at Disney only from time to time, this delicious treat tastes like a juicy caramel apple! The whiskey and lemonade are premixed in a slushy mixer at Disney Springs, so it cannot be ordered "virgin"; however, at home you can make it so if you'd like! Just substitute the apple whiskey with frozen apple juice concentrate.

SERVES 1

1½ cups lemonade, chilled, divided
2 ounces apple whiskey
½ cup whipped cream
1 teaspoon caramel sauce

1. Add 1 cup lemonade to an ice cube tray and freeze about 6 hours.

2. Add frozen lemonade cubes, remaining ½ cup lemonade, and apple whiskey to a blender and blend until slushy.

3. Serve in a large glass, topped with whipped cream and caramel sauce.

Fuzzy Tauntaun *(pictured)*

Oga's Cantina, Disneyland and Disney's Hollywood Studios

· · · ✦ · · ·

Watch out when you order or make this! The "fuzzy" part of the drink—the foam on top—has been known to numb tongues! It hasn't stopped park-goers from ordering it, though. In fact, the curiosity of the numbing foam has skyrocketed this drink to stardom. Guests pour into Oga's Cantina to taste for themselves the drink that is making waves on *Instagram*!

SERVES 1

1½ ounces peach vodka
¾ ounce peach schnapps
¾ ounce pulp-free orange-tangerine juice
¼ ounce Simple Syrup (see recipe in Chapter 2)
1 dollop Buzz Button Tingling Foam (see recipe in Chapter 2)

Shake all ingredients except Buzz Button Tingling Foam in a sealed cocktail shaker filled with ice. Strain into a tiki glass and top with Buzz Button Tingling Foam.

Grown-Up's Lemonade

Woody's Lunch Box, Disney's Hollywood Studios

· · · ✦ · · ·

Toy Story Land at Disney's Hollywood Studios exudes childhood. That's why the addition of a "Grown-Up's Lemonade" on the menu of Woody's Lunch Box is so unexpected and fun! Even grown-ups can enjoy feeling like kids again.

SERVES 1

½ cup frozen cherries, defrosted
½ cup lemonade
2 ounces cherry vodka
½ ounce Simple Syrup (see recipe in Chapter 2)
1 cup ice cubes

Add all ingredients except ice to a blender and blend until smooth. Serve in a highball glass over ice.

HippopotoMai-Tai

Trader Sam's Enchanted Tiki Bar, Disneyland Hotel

．．．＊．．．

The menu at Trader Sam's Enchanted Tiki Bar reads as follows for the HippopotoMai-Tai: "Dare to enter this hippo pool with...*Bang! Bang!* Two shots of rum! Don't worry. This drink is only dangerous when you start to wiggle your ears!" It refers to the famous scene in the Jungle Cruise where skippers fire two "shots" at the hippos that are about to charge. This drink is potent with two types of rum, so be sure you're ready for the *bang!*

SERVES 1

1 ounce white rum
1 ounce dark rum
½ ounce Orgeat (see recipe in Chapter 2)
½ ounce Agave Syrup (see recipe in Chapter 2)
½ ounce lime juice
¼ ounce dry curaçao
½ orange wheel
1 maraschino cherry
1 small sprig fresh mint

Add all ingredients except orange wedge, cherry, and mint sprig to a cocktail shaker filled with ice. Seal and shake ingredients to combine, then strain into a tiki or rocks glass filled with ice. Garnish with orange wheel on rim, maraschino cherry, and mint.

Hightower Rocks

Nomad Lounge, Disney's Animal Kingdom

* * * ✦ * * *

Like most drinks at Nomad Lounge, this one's name is a secret nod to an important person for those in the know. Imagineer Joe Rohde created most of Disney's Animal Kingdom and played a major role in the opening of Tiffins Restaurant and Nomad Lounge. His likeness was used for Harrison Hightower III, a corrupt explorer and star of Tokyo DisneySea's Tower of Terror attraction. This watermelony drink tips the hat to the two men who are one and the same: Hightower and Rohde.

SERVES 1

1½ ounces blanco tequila
1½ ounces watermelon juice
1½ ounces Simple Syrup
 (see recipe in Chapter 2)
½ ounce lemon juice
½ ounce lime juice
1 watermelon wedge, scored

Add all ingredients except watermelon wedge to a cocktail shaker filled with ice. Seal, shake, then pour into a rocks glass filled with ice. Garnish with watermelon wedge on rim.

Jedi Mind Trick

Oga's Cantina, Disneyland and Disney's Hollywood Studios

. . . ✦ . . .

This certainly *is* the drink you are looking for, no Jedi mind trick there! The grapefruity drink was named after the mystical protectors and practitioners of the Force, whose one great desire was to balance the powers of the galaxy. If you are looking for an out-of-this-world glass for this drink, try checking your local thrift stores. What's one person's trash is another person's treasure—and what was one person's 1990s cup might be your new Jedi Mind Trick glass!

SERVES 1

2 ounces grapefruit-rose vodka
1½ ounces Falernum (see recipe in Chapter 2)
1 ounce white grape juice
½ ounce blue curaçao
¼ ounce lime juice
⅛ teaspoon grapefruit bitters

Add all ingredients to a cocktail shaker filled with ice. Seal and shake, then strain over crushed ice in a large martini glass.

Krakatoa Punch

Trader Sam's Enchanted Tiki Bar, Disneyland Hotel

· · · ✦ · · ·

In a nod to the monstrous volcano whose eruption was heard around the world, this drink comes with a Disney glow cube that gives off the illusion of a volcano ready to burst. If you'd like to serve a glow cube with your home Krakatoa Punch, just search for "Disney glow ice cubes" online, and you'll find dozens of choices. This small detail can have an explosive effect on your presentation!

SERVES 1

1 ounce spiced rum
1 ounce dark rum
¾ ounce Hibiscus Grenadine
(see recipe in Chapter 2)
1 serving (6½ ounces) Sam's
Gorilla Grog (see recipe in
Chapter 2)

1. Shake all ingredients except Sam's Gorilla Grog in a sealed cocktail shaker filled with ice.

2. Pour Sam's Gorilla Grog into a tiki glass, then strain cocktail into glass. Add crushed ice to fill glass.

Nutty Irishman

The Hollywood Brown Derby, Disney's Hollywood Studios

· · · ✦ · · ·

If you've never had Frangelico before, it is like an Amaretto but is hazelnut instead of almond flavored. That's what puts the "nutty" in the Nutty Irishman! This restaurant exudes a vibe of old Hollywood elite, and if drinking this at home in your velvet robe doesn't make you feel like an A-lister, I don't know what will!

SERVES 1

1½ ounces Frangelico
1 ounce Irish cream liqueur
4 ounces hot coffee
½ cup canned whipped
cream

Pour all ingredients except whipped cream into a coffee mug. Top with whipped cream.

Jet Juice

Oga's Cantina, Disneyland and Disney's Hollywood Studios

• • • ✦ • • •

The Star Wars fan site *Wookieepedia* has entries for almost anything Star Wars related, including Jet Juice! Of this drink, the site states, "Jet Juice was a strong alcoholic beverage that was referred to as 'engine-room hooch' and could be brewed by pilots while in transit on starships. The manufacture of Jet Juice was officially banned by High Command of the Rebel Alliance; however, its creation and consumption was given a blind eye as long as it didn't interfere with one's duty." Well-known as one of the strongest drinks available at Oga's, guests continue to line up for a taste of this delicious "fuel."

SERVES 1

1½ ounces bourbon
¾ ounce Ancho Reyes ancho chile liqueur
½ ounce acai liqueur
½ ounce lemon juice
¼ ounce white grape juice

Add all ingredients to a cocktail shaker filled with ice, seal, and shake. Strain into a rocks glass.

DID YOU KNOW?

Star Wars: Galaxy's Edge in both Disneyland and Disney's Hollywood Studios is full of interactive elements. Download the Play Disney Parks app to your phone and have fun hacking into terminals throughout the Land. Through a series of activities, you'll learn your allegiance: Resistance, First Order, or smuggler!

La Cava Avocado

La Cava del Tequila, EPCOT

* * * ✦ * * *

La Cava del Tequila is located inside the "giant pyramid" in the Mexico pavilion of EPCOT. The whole space takes on the look of a Mexican night market, with the ceiling painted black with stars to imitate a clear night sky. Booths sell serapes and sombreros. La Cava del Tequila sells tequila flights, chips, and guacamole, but they are best known for their avocado margarita. This creamy drink has fresh avocado included for a funky new flavor you may have never tried before! Now you can enjoy this favorite at home.

SERVES 1

1 ounce blanco tequila
1 ounce Agave Syrup (see recipe in Chapter 2)
½ ounce lime juice
½ ounce Midori
¼ medium avocado, peeled and pitted
½ cup ice cubes
1 teaspoon Hibiscus Salt (see recipe in Chapter 2)
1 lime wedge, scored

1. Add all ingredients except Hibiscus Salt and lime wedge to a blender and blend until creamy.

2. Pour Hibiscus Salt into a shallow dish. Run lime wedge around the rim of a large martini glass, dip glass in Hibiscus Salt, and rotate to coat rim. Discard lime wedge.

3. Pour blended drink into rimmed glass.

DID YOU KNOW?

EPCOT used to have an interactive scavenger hunt called the "Kim Possible World Showcase Adventure." In the Mexico pavilion, your "Kimmunicator" would shoot evil Dr. Drakken out of the volcano on the back wall!

Ice Cream Martini

L'Artisan des Glaces, EPCOT

. . . ✦ . . .

Like everything at L'Artisan des Glaces, this martini is customizable! The following is a sample recipe of ingredients, but feel free to make these substitutions if you desire: Instead of whipped cream vodka, use Grand Marnier or rum. Instead of vanilla ice cream, try any ice cream or sorbet you like. Mix it up and combine *two* flavors! Every time you make this martini, it can be a new and different experience.

SERVES 1

1 ounce whipped cream vodka
½ cup vanilla ice cream

Pour vodka over ice cream in a large martini glass.

Jenn's Tattoo

Nomad Lounge, Disney's Animal Kingdom

. . . ✦ . . .

Back in Chapter 6, the drink Hibiscus Henna was introduced as the virgin, mocktail version of Jenn's Tattoo. So here we are: It's the cocktail version! Watermelon, hibiscus, and lime flavors, combined with vodka, create a fruity pop.

SERVES 1

1½ ounces vodka
1 ounce watermelon juice
½ ounce Hibiscus Grenadine (see recipe in Chapter 2)
¼ ounce lime juice
1 lime wheel, scored

Add all ingredients except lime wheel to a cocktail shaker filled with ice. Seal and shake, then strain into a rocks glass filled with ice. Garnish with lime wheel on rim.

Paradise Punch

Tambu Lounge, Disney's Polynesian Village Resort

· · · ✦ · · ·

Tangy and sweet flavors dominate this tiki beverage. The Ginger Syrup gives
a unique hint of flavor that sets this drink apart. Take your time to look around
Tambu Lounge if you get the chance to visit. It's a "pool bar" that has been
plunked down inside of a hotel! It even has its own thatched roof.
This drink is offered seasonally at Tambu Lounge.

SERVES 1

2 ounces passion-orange-
  guava juice
1 ounce spiced rum
1 ounce rye whiskey
1 ounce coconut water
¾ ounce Ginger Syrup (see
  recipe in Chapter 2)
¾ ounce lime juice
½ ounce blanco tequila
½ ounce pineapple juice
½ ounce cranberry juice
½ ounce grenadine

Add all ingredients to a cocktail shaker filled
with ice. Seal and shake, then strain into a
highball glass filled with ice.

S'mores Shake *(pictured)*

Beaches & Cream Soda Shop, Disney's Beach Club Resort

· · · ✦ · · ·

Beaches & Cream has served up delicious and over-the-top milkshakes ever since it opened at Disney's Beach Club Resort. But in 2016, everything changed when they started selling boozy floats and shakes for the adults to come and enjoy— and wow have they been popular! This shake has a rich and creamy flavor, thanks to the butterscotch tones of the Amarula.

SERVES 1

1½ cups vanilla ice cream
1½ cups chocolate ice cream
⅓ cup whole milk
¾ ounce crème de cacao
½ ounce Amarula
2 large marshmallows
1 graham cracker, crumbled
1 teaspoon chocolate sauce

1. Place ice creams, milk, crème de cacao, and Amarula in a blender. Blend until creamy.

2. Pour shake into a large drinking glass.

3. Skewer marshmallows. Using a kitchen torch, gently brown marshmallows, then place on top of shake. Garnish with graham cracker crumbs and chocolate sauce.

Stout Float

Beaches & Cream Soda Shop, Disney's Beach Club Resort

· · · ✦ · · ·

Just like the S'mores Shake, the Stout Float is part of the adult lineup at Beaches & Cream at Disney's Beach Club Resort. When you make this at home, feel free to use your favorite beer instead of Guinness. Different beers will result in a different flavor and body to the drink. It is basically a root beer float that is ready to party!

SERVES 1

¼ cup vanilla ice cream
1 (14.9-ounce) can Guinness stout
½ teaspoon chocolate sauce

Place ice cream in a 20-ounce glass. Top with Guinness. Drizzle with chocolate sauce.

Uh Oa!

Trader Sam's Enchanted Tiki Bar, Disneyland Hotel

. . . ✦ . . .

The Uh Oa! is more than just a drink: It is an experience. Insiders know that when you order this signature beverage off the menu at Trader Sam's Enchanted Tiki Bar, exciting things will happen! Bartenders and patrons alike will start to chant, "Uh Oa! Uh Oa!" to awaken the tiki goddess Uh Oa, who lives on the ceiling of the bar. Her eyes will light up, and you'll hear her ominous phrase: "When you mess with Polynesia, the tiki gods will squeeze ya!" The drink is also served on fire! (This version leaves flames to the professionals.) Complete the look by serving it in an official Disney tiki bowl (pictured).

SERVES 1

1 ounce white rum
1 ounce dark rum
1 ounce Falernum (see recipe in Chapter 2)
¾ ounce guava nectar
¾ ounce pulp-free orange juice
½ ounce grapefruit juice
½ ounce passion fruit juice
½ ounce pineapple juice
½ ounce lime juice
¹⁄₁₆ teaspoon ground cinnamon
1 maraschino cherry
1 lime wheel

Add all ingredients except cinnamon to a cocktail shaker filled with ice. Seal and shake, then strain into a tiki bowl or rocks glass filled with crushed ice. Sprinkle cinnamon on top and garnish with maraschino cherry and lime wheel.

Dessert Drinks

Let's finish off this sweet book with the sweetest chapter of all: Dessert Drinks. This chapter includes milkshakes, floats, and a couple of seasonal surprises. Pile up your own massive treats like they do at Black Tap with their CrazyShakes, slip away to your own private oasis while you try out a Dole Whip Float, or start new holiday traditions with the Pumpkin Spice Milkshake or an Elf Nog. However and whenever you decide to indulge in these decadent desserts, the spirit of Disney will permeate straight into your kitchen.

When making milkshakes, the outcome usually hinges on the quality of the ice cream you use. Be sure to pick a premium ice cream from the grocery store to use in your milkshakes, and the final product will be creamy and have a large depth of flavor. Even simple vanilla flavors vary greatly depending on the brand. Of course, making your own ice cream is always an excellent option. Get ready to mix up some delicious dessert drinks!

Black Forest Milkshake

Dockside Diner, Disney's Hollywood Studios

. . . ✦ . . .

Dockside Diner is an adorable little dinghy permanently docked in Echo Lake at Disney's Hollywood Studios. You can see the whole lake from this standpoint. Unfortunately, their offerings do seem to come and go with great frequency, so this Black Forest Milkshake may or may not be there the next time you visit. But now you've got this recipe on hand to make the shake whenever you want! The flavors in this milkshake are just like a decadent chocolate-covered cherry. It's sure to be a go-to!

SERVES 1

2½ cups vanilla ice cream
2 ounces cherry syrup
2 ounces whole milk
1 tablespoon dark chocolate sauce
½ cup whipped cream
1 maraschino cherry

1. Add ice cream, cherry syrup, and milk to a blender. Blend until smooth.

2. Stripe the inside of a clear 16-ounce plastic cup or glass with dark chocolate sauce. Pour milkshake into cup and top with whipped cream and maraschino cherry.

DID YOU KNOW?

The giant dinosaur that shares Echo Lake with Dockside Diner is named Gertie and was made to pay homage to one of the first animated characters ever, "Gertie the Trained Dinosaur," created by Winsor McCay in 1913. She even dons a Santa hat in the winter season!

Bam Bam Shake

Black Tap Craft Burgers & Shakes, Downtown Disney

* * * ✦ * * *

Black Tap is known for its over-the-top CrazyShakes, and this one is no exception. The original Fruity Pebbles cereal had the Flintstones as its mascots. Since this shake has Fruity Pebbles on the inside *and* outside, what name could be a better throwback to the family that started it all in the Stone Age?

SERVES 1

For Fruity Pebbles Bars
1 (10-ounce) bag mini
  marshmallows
3 tablespoons salted butter
3 cups Fruity Pebbles cereal
3 cups crisp rice cereal
1 cup powdered sugar
½ teaspoon vanilla extract
1½ tablespoons whole milk

For Shake
½ cup Fruity Pebbles cereal
3 cups vanilla ice cream
¼ cup whole milk

For Topping
2 tablespoons vanilla frosting
½ cup Fruity Pebbles cereal,
  divided
½ cup whipped cream
½ untoasted strawberry
  Pop-Tart
1 Laffy Taffy candy
1 maraschino cherry

1. To make Fruity Pebbles Bars: Line a 9" × 13" cake pan with parchment paper. Combine marshmallows and butter in a large microwave-safe bowl and microwave on high 2 minutes. Stir, then microwave an additional 1 minute. Stir well. Add Fruity Pebbles cereal and rice cereal and stir well. Scrape into prepared pan and flatten with a greased spatula. Allow to set 2 hours at room temperature.

2. Once set, cut into 2" × 4" bars. Place sugar, vanilla, and milk in a small dish and mix well. Use a spoon to drizzle icing over bars. Allow to set 30 minutes at room temperature.

3. To make Shake: Pour Fruity Pebbles cereal into a blender and pulse until consistency is a fine powder. Add ice cream and milk to blender and blend until smooth. Set aside.

4. To assemble: Coat top outer 1" of a tall milkshake glass in vanilla frosting and press ¼ cup Fruity Pebbles cereal into frosting. Pour milkshake into prepared glass. Top with whipped cream and sprinkle on remaining ¼ cup Fruity Pebbles. Place one Fruity Pebbles Bar, Pop-Tart, and Laffy Taffy in glass. Garnish with maraschino cherry.

Cosmic Cotton Candy Milkshake

Planet Hollywood, Disney Springs

* * * ✦ * * *

Black Tap isn't the only burger restaurant dishing out crazy shakes. Planet Hollywood took a page from their book when they created the Cosmic Cotton Candy Milkshake. Grab some soft pillows, whip up this yummy treat, put on your pajamas, and flip on your favorite movie. It's like being at Planet Hollywood, only better!

SERVES 1

3 tablespoons vanilla frosting
3 white chocolate-coated mini pretzels
2 tablespoons rainbow sprinkles
1 tablespoon chocolate syrup
¼ cup whole milk
1½ ounces cotton candy syrup
3 cups vanilla ice cream
½ cup whipped cream
½ cup cotton candy
1 round swirl lollipop

1. Prepare a glass pint jar by spreading vanilla frosting around top outer 3". Press pretzels and sprinkles into frosting. Drizzle chocolate syrup around inside of jar. Set aside.

2. Add milk, cotton candy syrup, and ice cream to a blender and blend until smooth. Pour into prepared jar. Top with whipped cream and cotton candy. Poke lollipop stick-end down into glass.

Caramel Apple Smoothie

Schmoozies!, Disney California Adventure

· · · ✳ · · ·

Calling this a "smoothie" is a bit of a stretch. Yes, it does contain fresh apples, which may categorize it as a smoothie. But Disney must have been trying to make this sound healthier than it is when they gave it that title! The amount of ice cream, milk, and caramel sauce pushes this drink over into milkshake territory. Try using other kinds of apples for a different flavor! This is a seasonal offering at Disney California Adventure during the fall months.

SERVES 1

4 tablespoons caramel sauce, divided
1 cup cored, peeled, and diced Granny Smith apples
½ cup whole milk
3 cups vanilla ice cream
½ cup whipped cream

1. Prepare a clear 16-ounce plastic cup or glass by drizzling 1 tablespoon caramel sauce around inside. Set aside.

2. Add apples, milk, ice cream, and 2 tablespoons caramel sauce to a blender and blend until smooth. Pour into prepared glass, top with whipped cream, and drizzle on remaining 1 tablespoon caramel sauce.

Brooklyn Blackout

Black Tap Craft Burgers & Shakes, Downtown Disney

. . . ✦ . . .

If you're a chocolate lover, this shake is for you. Named after the famous Blackout Cake created in Brooklyn, New York, at Ebinger Bakery, it contains copious amounts of chocolate. You can make the brownie fresh at home or buy it premade from the grocery store. You should never feel bad about buying store-bought finished ingredients for a dish. If it saves you time and sanity, it's worth doing! Both ways will accent this rich milkshake.

SERVES 1

2 tablespoons chocolate syrup, divided
2 tablespoons chocolate frosting
2 tablespoons mini milk chocolate chips
¼ cup whole milk
3 cups chocolate ice cream
1 large chocolate chunk brownie, halved diagonally
½ cup whipped cream

1. Prepare a tall milkshake glass by drizzling 1 tablespoon chocolate syrup around the inside. Spread frosting around top outer 2" of glass and press chocolate chips into frosting. Set aside.

2. Add milk and ice cream to a blender and blend until smooth. Pour into prepared glass. Place brownie triangles on top of glass, long side down. Top slices with whipped cream and drizzle on remaining 1 tablespoon chocolate syrup.

Cinnamon Sweet Churro Milkshake

Dockside Diner, Disney's Hollywood Studios

. . . ✦ . . .

Churro mania has really swept the world, and this is especially true at Disney Parks. Not even milkshakes are immune! This cinnamon-sugar shake is easy to make, contains ingredients you probably already have at home, and is superyummy! Refer to *The Unofficial Disney Parks Cookbook* for a homemade churro.

SERVES 1

2 teaspoons granulated sugar
1 teaspoon ground cinnamon
3 cups vanilla ice cream
¼ cup whole milk
½ cup whipped cream
1 churro

1. Mix sugar and cinnamon in a small bowl. Set aside. Add ice cream and milk to a blender and blend until smooth. Add cinnamon sugar and blend until well mixed.

2. Pour shake into a 16-ounce plastic cup or glass and top with whipped cream and churro.

Elf Nog

Hollywood Lounge, Disney California Adventure

. . . ✦ . . .

Feel free to adjust this winter offering to your liking. If the recipe comes out too thick for you, add more milk, ½ cup at a time, to provide a thinner consistency. Give or take on the nutmeg to your taste. Not into eggnog over ice? Lose the ice cubes. Making drinks at home means you can create exactly what you love!

SERVES 8

2 large eggs, well beaten
1 (14-ounce) can sweetened condensed milk
1 teaspoon vanilla extract
⅛ teaspoon salt
2 cups whole milk
1 cup heavy whipping cream
½ teaspoon ground nutmeg
8 cups ice cubes

Add all ingredients except ice to a pitcher and whisk together. Refrigerate until ready to use, up to 3 days. To serve, stir well, then pour over ice in eight regular drinking glasses.

Frozen Apple Pie

Appleseed Orchard, EPCOT

· · · ✦ · · ·

The World Showplace pavilion housed several small stations of snacks during the 2020 EPCOT International Food and Wine Festival. One of those booths represented Appleseed Orchard and served yummy apple-laced treats like the Frozen Apple Pie. It isn't a beverage so much as it is a whole dessert experience. Serve this with a straw and a spoon so you can eat the apple bits off the bottom and the streusel crumble off the top. The Red Delicious Apple Slush in the middle ties it all together.

SERVES 1

For Streusel Topping
1 tablespoon all-
  purpose flour
1 tablespoon granulated
  sugar
1 tablespoon light
  brown sugar
⅛ teaspoon ground
  cinnamon
⅛ teaspoon salt
1 tablespoon cold butter

For Apple Slush
4 ounces Red Delicious
  Apple Syrup (see
  recipe in Chapter 2)
1½ cups crushed ice

For Apple Pie Base
2 tablespoons diced
  apple pie filling

1. Preheat oven to 350°F. Grease an 8" × 8" baking dish with nonstick cooking spray or butter.

2. To make Streusel Topping: Combine all ingredients in a small bowl, using a fork or pastry cutter to cut cold butter into pebble-sized pieces while mixing. Pour mixture into prepared baking dish and bake 8 minutes or until golden brown. Allow to cool completely, about 30 minutes.

3. To make Apple Slush: Add Red Delicious Apple Syrup and ice to a blender and blend until smooth.

4. To assemble: Scoop Apple Pie Base into the bottom of a small plastic cup or glass. Pour Apple Slush over Apple Pie Base. Top with Streusel Topping. Serve with a spoon.

Dole Whip Float

Aloha Isle, Magic Kingdom

· · · ✦ · · ·

The debate rages on: Dole Whip cup, or Dole Whip Float?
The only difference is the addition of liquid pineapple juice to the float. Some find
this refreshing and an added bonus on a hot day. Others think the juice makes the
Dole Whip too sweet, too acidic, or too watered down. Give both a try and see
which camp you are going to pitch your tent in.

SERVES 1

For Dole Whip

1 cup water
1½ cups granulated
sugar
2 cups chilled pineapple
juice
1 tablespoon lime juice

For Float

1 cup chilled pineapple
juice

1. To make Dole Whip: In a medium microwave-safe bowl, combine water and sugar. Microwave 1 minute, stir, then microwave 1 more minute and stir to create a syrup. Cover and refrigerate at least 2 hours up to overnight.

2. Pour pineapple juice into a medium bowl and add ½ cup chilled syrup. Refrigerate remaining syrup up to 2 weeks. Add lime juice and stir. Pour into an ice cream machine. Follow manufacturer's instructions and run about 20 minutes or until creamy.

3. Scoop mixture into a medium sealable container and chill in freezer about 30 minutes or until slightly firm.

4. To make Float: Pour pineapple juice into a float glass and top with piped Dole Whip. Serve immediately.

Kakamora Floats

Aloha Isle, Magic Kingdom

· · · ✦ · · ·

Disney fans were first introduced to Kakamora when *Moana* hit the big screen in 2016. These adorable coconut creatures turn from cute to cutthroat when they try to steal the Heart of Te Fiti from Moana and Maui. A Kakamora now graces each Kakamora Float sold at Magic Kingdom in the form of a chocolate cake pop. Even without the cake pop, this float delivers in taste and presentation. The juices that form the base create a beautiful ombré effect that looks like a Polynesian sunset!

SERVES 2

For Kakamora Cake Pops

1 (15.25-ounce) box devil's food cake mix
1 cup water
½ cup vegetable oil
3 large eggs
5 cups semisweet chocolate chips, divided
1 (16-ounce) container chocolate frosting
1 cup white chocolate chips, divided
2 teaspoons black gel frosting

1. To make Kakamora Cake Pops: Preheat oven to 350°F. Mix together cake mix, water, oil, and eggs in a large bowl, then pour into a 9" × 13" cake pan lined with parchment paper. Bake 30 minutes or until a toothpick inserted in center comes out clean.

2. Allow cake to cool 5 minutes in pan, then crumble into a large bowl.

3. Pour 1 cup semisweet chocolate chips into crumbles and stir until melted and combined. Scoop frosting into bowl and mix well.

4. Line a baking sheet with parchment paper and use a 1.2-tablespoon cookie scoop to scoop cake into twelve balls, then place them on prepared sheet. Chill in freezer 10 minutes. Once chilled, shape into rounder balls.

5. Pour 1 cup semisweet chocolate chips into a medium microwave-safe container and microwave in 30-second increments until just melted. Dip the ends of Popsicle or long lollipop sticks into melted chocolate, then insert into cake balls. Return to freezer 30 minutes.

(continued) ▶

178

Peanut Butter and Jelly Milkshakes *(pictured)*

50's Prime Time Café, Disney's Hollywood Studios

· · · ✦ · · ·

Name a more iconic duo than peanut butter and jelly. I'll wait! This delicious pairing takes you back to the 1950s, when poodle skirts and jukeboxes were popular. If you aren't partial to grape jelly, feel free to substitute it with whatever flavor jelly you've got. You'll be rocking the sock hop while drinking this!

SERVES 2

3 cups vanilla ice cream
¼ cup whole milk
¼ cup creamy peanut butter
3 tablespoons grape jelly
2 maraschino cherries

Add all ingredients to a blender and blend until smooth. Pour into two tall milkshake glasses and top with maraschino cherries.

Pumpkin Spice Milkshake

Auntie Gravity's Galactic Goodies, Magic Kingdom

· · · ✦ · · ·

Pumpkin spice is a favorite coffee flavor of the fall, but Disney chefs asked, "What about a Pumpkin Spice Milkshake?" And we should all be glad they did, because this drink is *good*. Making it at home is especially convenient because you can adjust the amount of pumpkin syrup to your taste. Even if you live someplace that is still as hot as Hades in October, nothing could be more refreshing and in season than this milkshake!

SERVES 1

3 cups vanilla ice cream
¼ cup whole milk
1½ ounces pumpkin syrup
½ cup whipped cream
1 tablespoon caramel sauce
1 tablespoon Halloween
  sprinkles

Add ice cream, milk, and pumpkin syrup to a blender and blend until smooth. Pour into a 16-ounce plastic cup or glass. Top with whipped cream, drizzle on caramel sauce, and speckle with Halloween sprinkles.

Piña Colada Float

Marketplace Snacks, Disney Springs

· · · ✦ · · ·

A lot of people refer to this as a "Piña Colada Dole Whip," because it is basically that—a piña colada base topped with Dole Whip. This drink blasted onto the scene at Disney Springs in 2020 and became an *Instagram* sensation. It seems everyone loves the pineapple and coconut vibes it has to offer. You can make it at home and imagine you're on a shopping spree at Disney Springs!

SERVES 1

For Dole Whip
1 cup water
1½ cups granulated sugar
2 cups chilled pineapple juice
1 tablespoon lime juice

For Piña Colada
4 ounces nonalcoholic piña colada mix
2 ounces cream of coconut
2 cups crushed ice

1. To make Dole Whip: In a medium microwave-safe bowl, combine water and sugar. Microwave on high 1 minute, stir, then microwave 1 more minute and stir again to create a syrup. Cover and refrigerate at least 2 hours up to overnight.

2. Pour pineapple juice into a medium bowl and add ½ cup chilled syrup. (Remaining syrup can be covered and refrigerated up to 2 weeks.) Add lime juice and stir. Pour into an ice cream machine. Follow manufacturer's instructions and run about 20 minutes until creamy.

3. Scoop into a sealable container and chill in freezer about 30 minutes or until slightly firm.

4. To make Piña Colada: Add piña colada mix, cream of coconut, and ice to a blender and blend until smooth. Pour into a float cup and top with piped or scooped Dole Whip. Serve immediately.

Quake Shake

Ghirardelli Soda Fountain and Chocolate Shop, Disney Springs

* * * ✦ * * *

Time to get creative! When you order this drink at Disney Springs, a Ghirardelli worker will ask you to choose what kind of ice cream you want and to pick out three squares of Ghirardelli chocolates to flavor your shake. Choose among favorites like sea salt caramel, milk chocolate, dark chocolate, white chocolate, or peppermint bark. You can even choose three of the same flavor if you'd like! The result is a supercreamy milkshake with tiny sprinkles of chocolate blended in. Each sip has a wonderfully unique texture you're sure to love.

SERVES 1

¼ cup whole milk
3 cups ice cream
3 squares Ghirardelli
  chocolates of your choice
½ cup whipped cream

Add milk, ice cream, and chocolates to a blender. Blend until smooth. Pour into a 16-ounce plastic cup or glass and top with whipped cream. Serve immediately.

Peter Pan Floats

Storybook Treats, Magic Kingdom

. . . ✦ . . .

Playful and tart, this Disney fan favorite was brought back to Magic Kingdom after a short hiatus due to popular demand. Peter Pan's Flight can be found at both Disneyland and Walt Disney World, but the Magic Kingdom version has a beautiful queue that takes you through the Darling residence. Keep an eye out for Tinker Bell flitting around the room!

SERVES 10

For Drink

- 4 large egg yolks
- 2 large eggs
- 1¼ cups granulated sugar
- 1 tablespoon lemon juice
- ¾ cup lime juice
- 1¼ cups heavy whipping cream
- 1¼ cups whole milk
- 6 drops lime-green food coloring
- 2 liters lemon-lime soda

For Feather Garnish

- ¼ cup white chocolate chips
- 2 drops red gel food coloring

1. In a medium saucepan over medium heat, whisk together egg yolks, eggs, sugar, lemon juice, and lime juice. Cook 7 minutes, stirring continuously.

2. Strain mixture through a fine mesh sieve into a large bowl, discarding any solids. Add cream, milk, and food coloring. Stir to combine.

3. Refrigerate covered 1 hour.

4. Pour cooled mixture into an ice cream machine. Follow manufacturer's instructions and run about 20 minutes or until mixture begins to thicken. Scoop into a large sealable container, cover, and freeze 5 hours or overnight.

5. To make Feather Garnish: Heat chocolate in a small microwave-safe bowl on high 30 seconds. Stir, and microwave 30 seconds more. Repeat until chocolate just melts. Add food coloring and stir to combine. Smooth into a feather-shaped chocolate mold and refrigerate 1 hour or until hard.

6. To serve: Pour lemon-lime soda into ten float cups. Use a piping bag to swirl on ice cream, then top with Feather Garnish.

Poor Unfortunate Souls Float

Storybook Treats, Magic Kingdom

· · · ✦ · · ·

Few drinks are as divisive as this seasonal offering at Magic Kingdom. Some are weirded out by the idea of a cheese ice cream, while others find it delightful. Disney creators who came up with this float wanted to imitate the flavors of a berry pie and exude the character of *The Little Mermaid*'s Ursula. Make the crown sparkle with some edible shimmer spray, or use a chocolate crown mold instead of fondant. (Just melt ¼ cup white chocolate chips, mix with 2 drops yellow gel food coloring, and refrigerate in crown mold for 1 hour.)

SERVES 1

For Drink
6 ounces cream cheese, softened
¾ cup granulated sugar
1 tablespoon lemon juice
1 cup whole milk
¼ teaspoon salt
2 drops purple gel food coloring
1 drop black gel food coloring
1 cup heavy whipping cream
1 ounce Black Raspberry Syrup (see recipe in Chapter 2)
8 ounces Coca-Cola
1 tablespoon pearl sprinkles

For Crown Garnish
6 drops yellow gel food coloring
1 ounce (2 tablespoons) plain fondant

1. Add cream cheese, sugar, lemon juice, milk, salt, and food colorings to a blender and blend until well combined. Add whipping cream and stir gently to combine.

2. Pour mixture into an ice cream machine and run according to manufacturer's instructions 20 minutes or until creamy. Scoop into a large sealable container and freeze about 30 minutes.

3. Pour Black Raspberry Syrup and Coca-Cola into a float cup and stir gently to combine. Scoop ice cream into a piping bag with a star tip and swirl onto soda. Top with pearl sprinkles.

4. To make Crown Garnish: Add food coloring to fondant and knead until color is consistent. Roll out fondant, cut into a rectangle 1½" long, and cut crown points. Close together and let dry upright 1 hour. Once dry, place onto ice cream.

The Cake Shake

Black Tap Craft Burgers & Shakes, Downtown Disney

· · · ✦ · · ·

If you thought the cupcake on top of the Mickey Confetti Milkshake was extra, check this milkshake out: It has a whole slice of frosted birthday cake on top! The aptly named Cake Shake is not only topped with cake, but also has birthday cake mix in the shake. This may seem strange, but it creates an exceptionally smooth, distinct birthday cake flavor throughout. You could even try using different cake mixes to see what flavors you like best! This shake goes on and off the menu in Downtown Disney, but you can enjoy it at home anytime.

SERVES 1

2 tablespoons vanilla frosting
2 tablespoons rainbow sprinkles
3 cups vanilla ice cream
¼ cup whole milk
2 tablespoons white cake mix
1 slice frosted birthday cake
2 tablespoons whipped cream
1 maraschino cherry

1. Prepare a tall milkshake glass by spreading frosting around top outer 2". Press sprinkles onto frosting. Set aside.

2. Add ice cream, milk, and cake mix to a blender and blend until smooth. Pour into prepared glass. Place cake slice across rim of glass and top with whipped cream and maraschino cherry.

The Cookie Shake

Black Tap Craft Burgers & Shakes, Downtown Disney

· · · ✦ · · ·

Unlike The Cake Shake, The Cookie Shake has cookies as a garnish and contains a plain vanilla milkshake inside. It is like eating a plate of cookies with a glass of milk! This shake is both easy to make and stunning to look at. The piles of cookies and cookie crumbs on the outside of the glass are going to be snapped up by everyone at your next party right away!

SERVES 1

3 tablespoons vanilla frosting
9 small chocolate chip cookies, divided
2 tablespoons chocolate sauce, divided
3 cups vanilla ice cream
¼ cup whole milk
1 cup whipped cream

1. Prepare a tall milkshake glass by spreading frosting around top outer 3". Crush 3 cookies to crumbs and press crumbs into bottom 1" of frosting. Press 5 cookies into frosting around top 2". Drizzle 1 tablespoon chocolate sauce around inside of glass. Set aside.

2. Add ice cream and milk to a blender and blend until smooth. Pour into prepared glass. Top with whipped cream. Crush remaining cookie and sprinkle crumbs on whipped cream, and drizzle with remaining 1 tablespoon chocolate sauce.

Strawberry Shortcake CrazyShake

Black Tap Craft Burgers & Shakes, Downtown Disney

· · · ✳ · · ·

Yum yum! Fresh strawberries add a pop of fruity flavor to this milkshake. If you live someplace where strawberries are ripe in the summertime, try to find a local farm where you can pick your own berries. That way you'll have the ripest and freshest strawberries to add to this delicious concoction.

SERVES 1

2 tablespoons vanilla frosting
3 tablespoons crumbled shortcake, divided
1 cup hulled and diced fresh strawberries
¼ cup whole milk
4 tablespoons strawberry syrup, divided
3 cups vanilla ice cream
1 strawberry shortcake ice cream bar
½ cup whipped cream
1 maraschino cherry

1. Prepare a tall milkshake glass by spreading frosting around top outer 1". Press 2 tablespoons crumbled shortcake into frosting. Set aside.

2. Add strawberries, milk, 1 tablespoon strawberry syrup, and ice cream to a blender and blend until smooth. Pour into prepared glass.

3. Place strawberry shortcake bar, tip down, into shake. Top with whipped cream, sprinkle on remaining 1 tablespoon shortcake crumbles, and drizzle on remaining 3 tablespoons strawberry syrup. Top with maraschino cherry.

MIX IT UP

This milkshake can be made with frozen strawberries instead of fresh. Just let them thaw before using them to ensure they blend entirely into the shake.

The Headless Horseman Rides Again Floats

Sunshine Tree Terrace, Magic Kingdom

· · · ✦ · · ·

This seasonal Halloween treat can now be enjoyed year-round in your home! I can think of no better summertime sweet than a strawberry-ice-cream-and-soda float. This drink is named as such because it comes with a crazy straw and a keychain of the Headless Horseman himself.

SERVES 2

2 cups hulled and sliced fresh strawberries
2 cups strawberry Fanta soda, divided
½ cup heavy whipping cream
1 cup granulated sugar

1. Add strawberries and 1 cup Fanta to a blender and blend until smooth. Strain into a large bowl and discard solids.

2. Add cream and sugar to strawberry mix and whisk. Pour carefully into an ice cream machine and run according to manufacturer's instructions 20 minutes or until semisolid.

3. Divide remaining 1 cup Fanta into two float glasses. Scoop ice cream into a piping bag with a large star tip and squeeze over Fanta in glasses. Serve immediately.

MIXING TIP

If you don't have a piping bag with a star tip (or just don't want to bother with one), feel free to use an ice cream scoop to make your floats. It's easier and less messy!

Disney Parks
Drink Locations

Interested in where each of the drinks in Part 2 can be found at the Disney Parks? Hoping to grab an original Blue Milk and test it against your re-creation during your next visit? Use the following maps to discover where you can find each of the more than one hundred drinks in Part 2!

You'll discover a map for each of the following magical locations: Disneyland, Star Wars: Galaxy's Edge, Magic Kingdom, EPCOT, Disney's Hollywood Studios, Disney's Animal Kingdom, and Disney California Adventure. You may notice that Galaxy's Edge has a separate map here, while it is not one of the six main US parks. It is actually a part of both California's Disneyland and Orlando's Hollywood Studios. So why does it get its own map? Because there are so many delicious recipes from Part 2 located at this great part of the main parks! I wanted to make sure it would be easy to determine just where each drink can be found.

Each map includes a numbered key, so you can match a star on the map to what drink is found there, as well as what chapter of this book the recipe for that drink can be found in. You will also notice there are three different-colored stars on the Galaxy's Edge map: yellow, red, and blue. A yellow star means that drink is available at both the Disneyland and Disney's Hollywood Studios Galaxy's Edge locations. A red star means that drink is only available at the Disneyland Galaxy's Edge location. A blue star means that drink is only available at the Hollywood Studios Galaxy's Edge location. Read on to check it out for yourself!

Some drinks are found at resorts, hotels, or entertainment districts that are technically outside of the parks themselves. A list of these drinks and the locations where they can be enjoyed is provided in the Resort, Hotel, and Entertainment District Drink Location Key at the end of this book.

STAR WARS:
GALAXY'S EDGE

CRITTER COUNTRY

FRONTIERLAND

NEW ORLEANS
SQUARE

2

ADVENTURELAND

MAIN STREET, U.S.A

FANTASYLAND

TOMORROWLAND

SEE GALAXY'S EDGE MAP, ON PAGES: 200–201

DISNEYLAND

1 **JUNGLE JULEP** *(Adventureland, Disneyland, Chapter 4: Slushes)*

2 **NEW ORLEANS MINT JULEP** *(New Orleans Square, Disneyland, Chapter 6: Mocktails)*

GALAXY'S EDGE

FRONTIERLAND

LIBERTY SQUARE

ADVENTURELAND

MAIN STREET, U.S.A.

MAGIC KINGDOM

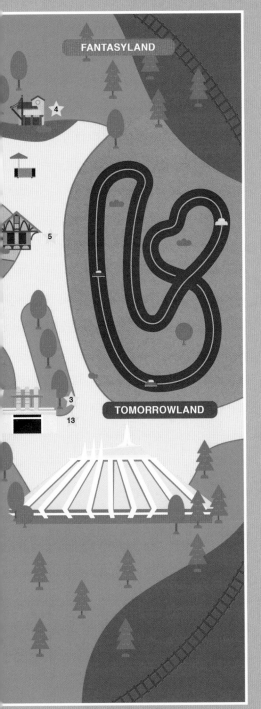

1   **LEFOU'S BREW** *(Fantasyland, Magic Kingdom, Chapter 4: Slushes)*

2   **PIRATE PEAR SLUSHY** *(Adventureland, Magic Kingdom, Chapter 4: Slushes)*

3   **SPACE RANGER SLUSHIES** *(Tomorrowland, Magic Kingdom, Chapter 4: Slushes)*

4   **WITCH'S FROZEN BREW** *(Fantasyland, Magic Kingdom, Chapter 4: Slushes)*

5   **WONDERLAND SLUSHY** *(Fantasyland, Magic Kingdom, Chapter 4: Slushes)*

6   **FROZEN CAPPUCCINOS** *(Main Street, U.S.A., Magic Kingdom, Chapter 5: Coffee, Tea, Hot Chocolate, & Cider)*

7   **HOT HOLIDAY CIDER** *(Main Street, U.S.A., Magic Kingdom, Chapter 5: Coffee, Tea, Hot Chocolate, & Cider)*

8   **PUNCH LINE PUNCH** *(Adventureland, Magic Kingdom, Chapter 6: Mocktails)*

9   **DOLE WHIP FLOAT** *(Adventureland, Magic Kingdom, Chapter 8: Dessert Drinks)*

10   **KAKAMORA FLOATS** *(Adventureland, Magic Kingdom, Chapter 8: Dessert Drinks)*

11   **PETER PAN FLOATS** *(Fantasyland, Magic Kingdom, Chapter 8: Dessert Drinks)*

12   **POOR UNFORTUNATE SOULS FLOAT** *(Fantasyland, Magic Kingdom, Chapter 8: Dessert Drinks)*

13   **PUMPKIN SPICE MILKSHAKE** *(Tomorrowland, Magic Kingdom, Chapter 8: Dessert Drinks)*

14   **THE HEADLESS HORSEMAN RIDES AGAIN FLOATS** *(Adventureland, Magic Kingdom, Chapter 8: Dessert Drinks)*

GERMANY

ITALY

THE AMERICAN
ADVENTURE

CHINA

MEXICO

FUTURE WORLD
EAST

ENTRANCE

EPCOT

1 BLOOD ORANGE ACQUA FRESCA
(Italy, EPCOT, Chapter 3: Lemonades & Fruity Drinks)

2 BLOOD ORANGE (VIRGIN) MIMOSA *(Port of Entry, EPCOT, Chapter 3: Lemonades & Fruity Drinks)*

3 MIXED BERRIES DELIGHT *(Morocco, EPCOT, Chapter 3: Lemonades & Fruity Drinks)*

4 STRAWBERRY ACQUA FRESCA
(Italy, EPCOT, Chapter 3: Lemonades & Fruity Drinks)

5 THE RED MAPLE *(Canada, EPCOT, Chapter 3: Lemonades & Fruity Drinks)*

6 TROPICAL BREEZE SMOOTHIE *(Morocco, EPCOT, Chapter 3: Lemonades & Fruity Drinks)*

7 POMEGRANATE-LIME FROZEN VIRGIN MOJITO *(Mexico, EPCOT, Chapter 4: Slushes)*

8 HABIBI DAIQUIRI
(Morocco, EPCOT, Chapter 4: Slushes)

9 MOROCCARITA
(Morocco, EPCOT, Chapter 4: Slushes)

10 ROYAL BLUE *(Morocco, EPCOT, Chapter 4: Slushes)*

11 SULTAN'S COLADA
(Morocco, EPCOT, Chapter 4: Slushes)

12 THE AMERICAN DREAM
(The American Adventure, EPCOT, Chapter 4: Slushes)

13 VIOLET LEMONADE *(Port of Entry, EPCOT, Chapter 4: Slushes)*

14 BUBBLE MILK TEA *(China, EPCOT, Chapter 5: Coffee, Tea, Hot Chocolate, & Cider)*

15 ESPRESSO GELATO AFFOGATO *(Italy, EPCOT, Chapter 5: Coffee, Tea, Hot Chocolate, & Cider)*

16 LA CAVA AVOCADO *(Mexico, EPCOT, Chapter 7: Cocktails)*

17 ICE CREAM MARTINI *(France, EPCOT, Chapter 7: Cocktails)*

18 FROZEN APPLE PIE *(World Showplace Pavilion, EPCOT, Chapter 8: Dessert Drinks)*

19 FROZEN S'MORE *(World Showplace Pavilion, EPCOT, Chapter 8: Dessert Drinks)*

STAR WARS:
GALAXY'S EDGE

2
8

5

AN INCREDIBLE
CELEBRATION

COMMISSARY LANE

6

3

10

11

ECHO LAKE

7
9

1

12

HOLLYWOOD BOULEVARD

ENTRANCE

TOY STORY LAND

ANIMATION COURTYARD

SUNSET BOULEVARD

SEE GALAXY'S EDGE
MAP, ON PAGES: 200–201

DISNEY'S HOLLYWOOD STUDIOS

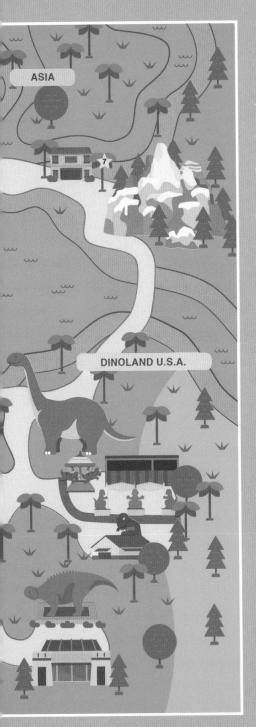

DISNEY'S ANIMAL KINGDOM

1. **BIBO** *(Africa, Disney's Animal Kingdom, Chapter 3: Lemonades & Fruity Drinks)*

2. **FROZEN FLAMINGO** *(Africa, Disney's Animal Kingdom, Chapter 3: Lemonades & Fruity Drinks)*

3. **PANDORAN SUNRISE** *(Pandora—The World of Avatar, Disney's Animal Kingdom, Chapter 3: Lemonades & Fruity Drinks)*

4. **SPARBERRY SODA** *(Africa, Disney's Animal Kingdom, Chapter 3: Lemonades & Fruity Drinks)*

5. **SPOOKY APPLE PUNCH** *(Discovery Island, Disney's Animal Kingdom, Chapter 3: Lemonades & Fruity Drinks)*

6. **NIGHT BLOSSOM** *(Pandora—The World of Avatar, Disney's Animal Kingdom, Chapter 4: Slushes)*

7. **SHANGRI-LA BERRY FREEZE** *(Asia, Disney's Animal Kingdom, Chapter 4: Slushes)*

8. **FRENCH VANILLA ICED COFFEE** *(Discovery Island, Disney's Animal Kingdom, Chapter 5: Coffee, Tea, Hot Chocolate, & Cider)*

9. **HIBISCUS HENNA** *(Discovery Island, Disney's Animal Kingdom, Chapter 6: Mocktails)*

10. **KIAMA MAMMA** *(Discovery Island, Disney's Animal Kingdom, Chapter 6: Mocktails)*

11. **LILLY GORILL-IE** *(Discovery Island, Disney's Animal Kingdom, Chapter 6: Mocktails)*

12. **ZINGIBER FIZZIE** *(Discovery Island, Disney's Animal Kingdom, Chapter 6: Mocktails)*

13. **HIGHTOWER ROCKS** *(Discovery Island, Disney's Animal Kingdom, Chapter 7: Cocktails)*

14. **JENN'S TATTOO** *(Discovery Island, Disney's Animal Kingdom, Chapter 7: Cocktails)*

CARS LAND

PACIFIC WHARF

1

HOLLYWOOD LAND

7

9

2

3

5

6

8

BUENA VISTA STREET

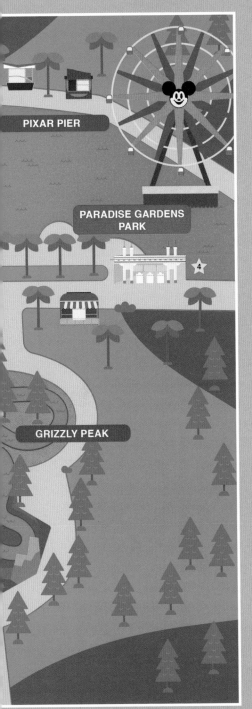

DISNEY CALIFORNIA ADVENTURE

1. **RAMONE'S "PEAR OF DICE" SODA** (Cars Land, Disney California Adventure, Chapter 3: Lemonades & Fruity Drinks)

2. **MY BUGS! MY BUGS!** (Hollywood Land, Disney California Adventure, Chapter 4: Slushes)

3. **SLEIGH-RIDE SLUSH** (Hollywood Land, Disney California Adventure, Chapter 4: Slushes)

4. **ABUELITA HOT COCOA** (Paradise Gardens Park, Disney California Adventure, Chapter 5: Coffee, Tea, Hot Chocolate, & Cider)

5. **WINTER HOT CHOCOLATE** (Hollywood Land, Disney California Adventure, Chapter 5: Coffee, Tea, Hot Chocolate, & Cider)

6. **GHOULISH DELIGHT** (Hollywood Land, Disney California Adventure, Chapter 6: Mocktails)

7. **CARAMEL APPLE SMOOTHIE** (Hollywood Land, Disney California Adventure, Chapter 8: Dessert Drinks)

8. **ELF NOG** (Hollywood Land, Disney California Adventure, Chapter 8: Dessert Drinks)

9. **MINNIE WITCH SHAKE** (Hollywood Land, Disney California Adventure, Chapter 8: Dessert Drinks)

Resort, Hotel, and Entertainment District Drink Location Key

DISNEYLAND HOTEL

1 **HIPPOPOTOMAI-TAI** *(Chapter 7: Cocktails)*

2 **KRAKATOA PUNCH** *(Chapter 7: Cocktails)*

3 **UH OA!** *(Chapter 7: Cocktails)*

DOWNTOWN DISNEY DISTRICT

1 **BAM BAM SHAKE**
(Chapter 8: Dessert Drinks)

2 **BROOKLYN BLACKOUT**
(Chapter 8: Dessert Drinks)

3 **STRAWBERRY SHORTCAKE CRAZYSHAKE** *(Chapter 8: Dessert Drinks)*

4 **THE CAKE SHAKE**
(Chapter 8: Dessert Drinks)

5 **THE COOKIE SHAKE**
(Chapter 8: Dessert Drinks)

DISNEY'S POLYNESIAN VILLAGE RESORT

1 **KEIKI LEMONADE**
(Chapter 3: Lemonades & Fruity Drinks)

2 **POMEGRANATE LEMONADE**
(Chapter 3: Lemonades & Fruity Drinks)

3 **POLYNESIAN PUNCH**
(Chapter 6: Mocktails)

4 **SCHWEITZER FALLS**
(Chapter 6: Mocktails)

5 **SPARKLING NO-JITO** *(Chapter 6: Mocktails)*

6 **SKIPPER SIPPER** *(Chapter 6: Mocktails)*

7 **PARADISE PUNCH** *(Chapter 7: Cocktails)*

DISNEY'S BEACH CLUB RESORT

1 **FROZEN SUNSHINE**
(Chapter 3: Lemonades & Fruity Drinks)

2 **S'MORES SHAKE** *(Chapter 7: Cocktails)*

3 **STOUT FLOAT** *(Chapter 7: Cocktails)*

4 **MICKEY CONFETTI MILKSHAKE**
(Chapter 8: Dessert Drinks)

DISNEY'S BOARDWALK

1 **COTTON CANDY LEMONADE**
(Chapter 3: Lemonades & Fruity Drinks)

2 **LAVA SMOOTHIE**
(Chapter 3: Lemonades & Fruity Drinks)

3 **HOODUNIT'S PUNCH** *(Chapter 6: Mocktails)*

4 **VIRGIN MAGIC MIRROR**
(Chapter 6: Mocktails)

DISNEY'S CARIBBEAN BEACH RESORT

1 **THE PEACHCOMBER**
(Chapter 6: Mocktails)

2 **TROPICAL PARADISE**
(Chapter 6: Mocktails)

DISNEY'S ANIMAL KINGDOM LODGE

1 **JUNGLE JUICE**
(Chapter 3: Lemonades & Fruity Drinks)

DISNEY SPRINGS

1 **POPPING YUZU LEMONADE**
(Chapter 3: Lemonades & Fruity Drinks)

2 **GOOFY'S GLACIER** *(Chapter 4: Slushes)*

3 **HOT CHOCOLATE AFFOGATO** *(Chapter 5: Coffee, Tea, Hot Chocolate, & Cider)*

4 **TEDDY'S TEA** *(Chapter 5: Coffee, Tea, Hot Chocolate, & Cider)*

5 **DIVING BELL** *(Chapter 6: Mocktails)*

6 **POISONLESS DART** *(Chapter 6: Mocktails)*

7 **CANADIAN APPLE SLUSHY**
(Chapter 7: Cocktails)

8 **COSMIC COTTON CANDY MILKSHAKE**
(Chapter 8: Dessert Drinks)

9 **PIÑA COLADA FLOAT**
(Chapter 8: Dessert Drinks)

10 **QUAKE SHAKE** *(Chapter 8: Dessert Drinks)*

DISNEY'S GRAND CALIFORNIAN HOTEL & SPA

1 **HOT SPICED APPLE CIDER**
(Chapter 5: Coffee, Tea, Hot Chocolate, & Cider)

MULTIPLE LOCATIONS

1 **INCREDIBLE FROZEN FLAME**
(Chapter 4: Slushes)

2 **CINDERELLA LATTE**
(Chapter 5: Coffee, Tea, Hot Chocolate, & Cider)

3 **PUMPKIN PIE LATTE**
(Chapter 5: Coffee, Tea, Hot Chocolate, & Cider)

4 **SHAKIN' JAMAICAN COLD BREW**
(Chapter 5: Coffee, Tea, Hot Chocolate, & Cider)

5 **TOFFEE FLIGHT HOT CHOCOLATE**
(Chapter 5: Coffee, Tea, Hot Chocolate, & Cider)

Standard US/Metric Measurement Conversions

VOLUME CONVERSIONS	
US Volume Measure	**Metric Equivalent**
⅛ teaspoon	0.5 milliliter
¼ teaspoon	1 milliliter
½ teaspoon	2 milliliters
1 teaspoon	5 milliliters
½ tablespoon	7 milliliters
1 tablespoon (3 teaspoons)	15 milliliters
2 tablespoons (1 fluid ounce)	30 milliliters
¼ cup (4 tablespoons)	60 milliliters
⅓ cup	90 milliliters
½ cup (4 fluid ounces)	125 milliliters
⅔ cup	160 milliliters
¾ cup (6 fluid ounces)	180 milliliters
1 cup (16 tablespoons)	250 milliliters
1 pint (2 cups)	500 milliliters
1 quart (4 cups)	1 liter (about)
WEIGHT CONVERSIONS	
US Weight Measure	**Metric Equivalent**
½ ounce	15 grams
1 ounce	30 grams
2 ounces	60 grams
3 ounces	85 grams
¼ pound (4 ounces)	115 grams
½ pound (8 ounces)	225 grams
¾ pound (12 ounces)	340 grams
1 pound (16 ounces)	454 grams

OVEN TEMPERATURE CONVERSIONS

Degrees Fahrenheit	Degrees Celsius
200 degrees F	95 degrees C
250 degrees F	120 degrees C
275 degrees F	135 degrees C
300 degrees F	150 degrees C
325 degrees F	160 degrees C
350 degrees F	180 degrees C
375 degrees F	190 degrees C
400 degrees F	205 degrees C
425 degrees F	220 degrees C
450 degrees F	230 degrees C

BAKING PAN SIZES

American	Metric
8 × 1½ inch round baking pan	20 × 4 cm cake tin
9 × 1½ inch round baking pan	23 × 3.5 cm cake tin
11 × 7 × 1½ inch baking pan	28 × 18 × 4 cm baking tin
13 × 9 × 2 inch baking pan	30 × 20 × 5 cm baking tin
2 quart rectangular baking dish	30 × 20 × 3 cm baking tin
15 × 10 × 2 inch baking pan	30 × 25 × 2 cm baking tin (Swiss roll tin)
9 inch pie plate	22 × 4 or 23 × 4 cm pie plate
7 or 8 inch springform pan	18 or 20 cm springform or loose bottom cake tin
9 × 5 × 3 inch loaf pan	23 × 13 × 7 cm or 2 lb narrow loaf or pâté tin
1½ quart casserole	1.5 liter casserole
2 quart casserole	2 liter casserole

Index

About the Author

As a child who grew up in Anaheim Hills, California, ASHLEY CRAFT could recite the Star Tours ride by heart and navigate the park without a map, and she fell asleep to the sound of Disneyland fireworks each night in her bedroom. After two internships at Walt Disney World and many, many more visits to the Disney Parks, Ashley is now one of the leading experts on Disneyland and Walt Disney World. Her popular blog, *AshleyCrafted*, is best known for featuring recipes inspired by Disney Park foods to help people re-create that Disney magic right in their own kitchens. Her first book, *The Unofficial Disney Parks Cookbook*, became an instant bestseller. Add her on *Instagram* @ashley.crafted.

EVEN MORE MAGIC OF DISNEY— IN YOUR KITCHEN!

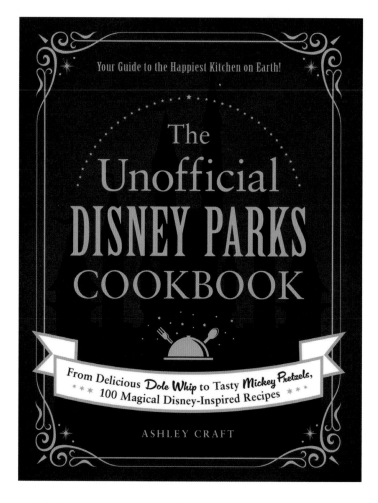

Your Guide to the Happiest Kitchen on Earth!

The
Unofficial
DISNEY PARKS
COOKBOOK

From Delicious *Dole Whip* to Tasty *Mickey Pretzels*, 100 Magical Disney-Inspired Recipes

ASHLEY CRAFT

Pick Up or Download Your Copy Today!

adamsmedia
An Imprint of Simon & Schuster
A ViacomCBS COMPANY